home
furnishing
with fabric

home furnishing
with fabric

Leslie Geddes-Brown

with step-by-step projects by **Lucinda Ganderton**

RYLAND
PETERS
& SMALL
London   New York

Senior designer **Sally Powell**

Senior editor **Henrietta Heald**

Location research manager **Kate Brunt**

Location researcher **Sarah Hepworth**

Picture researcher **Jenny Drane**

Production **Patricia Harrington**

Art director **Gabriella Le Grazie**

Publishing director **Alison Starling**

Illustration **Lizzie Sanders**

Specially commissioned photography

David Montgomery; styling **Serena Hanbury**

Index **Alison Bravington**

First published in the USA in 2001

by Ryland Peters & Small Inc.

519 Broadway

5th Floor

New York, NY 10012

www.rylandpeters.com

10 9 8 7 6 5 4 3 2 1

ISBN 1 84172 168 9

Printed and bound in China

contents

introduction

Take a plain cube of a room. Paint it a soft neutral gray, with matt-white ceiling, door, and baseboards, and more of the same on the frames of the traditional sash windows. The floor is made of softly polished wood. Here is a perfect space in which to experiment with what fabrics can do for a room.

You want to be minimalist? Add a pair of leather Wassily chairs designed by Marcel Breuer in 1925, a fireplace carved halfway up the wall, a set of Rupert Spira pots and, on the wall, a Yoruba narrowstrip textile in ocher, terracotta, black, and dark vermilion.

Swedish? Put in a curved hardback settle with cabriole legs, and cover it with square cushions in pink and gray stripes and checks. Put a round-bellied longcase clock against one wall and, at the windows, hang sheer white linens in front of shades in a variation on the pink and grey cushions.

For a French room, you could substitute gilded fauteuils and change the clock for a wood and ormolu pillar timepiece on a bracket. Instead of checks and stripes, the chairs could be upholstered in rose-madder toile de Jouy and the windows given generous curtains of the same pictorial cotton backed by a checked toile de Nîmes.

An English Regency room would return to generous stripes—but, unlike the Swedish cottons, these would be silk twill in vibrant colors—black and ultramarine, citrus yellow with scarlet, purple and emerald green. The furniture, upholstered in shades of these colors, or embroidered with gros and petit point, would be saber-legged and brass-inlaid, perhaps including a chaise longue with plain silk bolster. The walls would be densely hung with silk-embroidered pictures of flowers and butterflies, and the curtains swagged, tasseled and valanced with gilded arrow poles.

That same experimental cube could become a vernacular American parlor, where a traditional log-cabin quilt hangs on the wall behind a painted chest of drawers adorned with a single decoy. The curtains are a strong tweed check in design, but made of cotton woven in browns and grays. Cushions on the hardback chairs are in one of the brown pictorial cottons—closely resembling toile, but showing a glorious scene from the Mexican–American war. There's a rag rug on the floor decorated with the Stars and Stripes.

It's tempting to go on, through Japanese- and Chinese-inspired rooms, to those instigated by India and Africa, by Russia and Italy. But you get the point: a room is only an architectural space if it has no furnishings or fabrics. It only becomes a proper room—your own creation—when fabric furnishings are added. They are as important as that.

FABRIC STYLES

From soft neutrals to joyful toiles, from crisp cotton to luscious damask—what gives a room its character, what can change it utterly, is the choice of fabric and how you use it.

solid colors

Unlike patterns, solid fabrics virtually never go out of fashion—though the colors you choose just may. The secret is to pick complex mixtures of shades and tones or to vary the textures. If your colors are strong or rich, forget about texture; if they are refined and subtle, look for interesting weaves and slubs.

At the opposite end of the color spectrum from neutral, solid fabrics ask for the sort of strong colors and color combinations that have become the hallmark of designers of today. Such professionals would be the first to tell you that achieving results in this area is far from easy. It all depends on color saturations, levels of blues mixed with reds or reds with yellows. But the theory doesn't really matter. The best way to make sure these thugs in the color spectrum behave for you is to mix them together on a color board and spend days looking at how they work in different lights, in different moods, and in different mixtures.

Large areas of strong color, whether black or chocolate, cerise or tangerine, are the hardest to get right—but with thought and experiment it can be done. Remember that the larger the area of one color—vermilion curtains on deep sash windows, for instance—the more the color will take over. It may set up reactions with other shades around it, shadowing blues

OPPOSITE PAGE, LEFT There is only one patterned fabric in this elegant room. The startling zebra stripes contrast with the sleek gray sofa and the minimalist lamp and rug.

OPPOSITE PAGE, RIGHT If you think solid colors are boring, just consider this stunning mixture of soft fruit: raspberry mixed with redcurrant, with a touch of whitecurrant coloring in the burlap detail on the pillows and in the ropes on the back of the sofa.

LEFT Bold ultramarine holds this charming bedroom together. The checked and striped pillows match the chair's upholstery exactly, and the same shade is picked up in the pretty patchwork quilt that covers the bed.

BELOW This Paris living room relies for its decorative effect on salvaged wood and utterly plain colors. But the combination of off-black, off-white, and crimson has a strong abstract quality.

into indistinct mauve, making white walls come over pink. If you want to take this brave course, you may even have to make changes at the last minute. One solution is to proceed one step at a time: find the right red or the right yellow, but use it in small amounts—pillows, throws, accessories—until you are sure you have got it perfect. Buy a length of solid fabric and drape it around the window to get the effect of curtains

FAR LEFT This relaxed room manages to integrate the interior and exterior of the house by using soft greens and floral cotton pillows on the sofa in front of the window. All the colors in the room are in keeping with the features that are visible in the garden.
LEFT It is not a God-given rule that chairs in a dining room should match each other. But this disparate quartet around a table are all upholstered in shades of green that appear elsewhere in the room.

or over the armchairs to see how it would look as slipcovers. Be ready to tone down the brightness of your walls and remove all clutter, from small paintings to shelves of books, to achieve the right clarity for your big statement. For big statement this will be. Get it right, and the results will be stunning. Wrong—and the stunning effect will be like a thump on the head and stars circling around the eyes.

Personally, I think it is worth being brave, particularly so if you have a well-proportioned room with good light (views don't matter). Strong colors are also helpful for people who dislike clutter or, for that matter, cannot afford a great deal of furniture. A chair or two covered with scarlet cotton throws, windows framed with bright but unpatterned sari silks, a single green leaf in a vase, and one large picture in colors that bring together the entire scheme are all that is needed here.

You can add in any number of neutral shades such as string and cement—they will simply give reassurance. However, if you were to throw a single vermilion pillow into your subtle white-on-white room, it would be like adding a tomato into a basketful of eggs—exciting, but not what you originally intended. The best combinations of colors are often discovered by accident. Try moving cushions, throws, and rugs from room to room to see if you can come up with the unexpected.

neutrals and plain weaves

The move toward solid fabrics plainly woven is a reaction to the power-shouldered curtain treatments of the 1980s, when fortunes were spent on buying luxury silk and damask in such lengths that they trailed uselessly on the floor. The urge to decorate in a succession of neutral shades—bone, string, greige, stone, mouse—followed.

ABOVE This is a highly sophisticated scheme that matches the subtlest shades of gray and off-white with bland steel furniture and the neutrals of blond wood and canework. The textures in the room come from the natural wood and willow.
ABOVE RIGHT The cream and white linens covering the sofas match the vellum on the living-room wall. Everything is restrained except for the two pillows, whose inclusion draws each element together.
RIGHT Fashion fabrics from Donegal, including linens and tweeds, have been used to make throws, cushions, and covers for an elegant Parisian living room.

Is it a coincidence that the word "fash"—meaning "bother, inconvenience, trouble"—appears directly before "fashion" in my dictionary? If so, it is perfectly appropriate. In interiors as much as in clothes, fashion is an inconvenience that should, if possible, be avoided. It may not be possible to ignore fashion entirely, but anyone who wants a calm, pleasant, and less extravagant life should try to disregard the fads of the moment and look instead at the direction in which the mainstream is leading. Fashion in fabric furnishings is much the same as that in clothes: the taste-makers are looking for innovations, which only they are aware of, while the mass of people trust the big advertisers and the big stores to point them in the right direction—by which time the fashion has usually gone cold.

For several years now, the cognoscenti have been hanging old French linen bedsheets instead of curtains. Stained, patched, amateurishly embroidered in cross-stitch in inconvenient places, these sheets are made of handwoven fabric; the yarn itself is handspun, and even the hems are hand-sewn. This style of material, found only in the most eclectic antique shops for far less money than a designer fabric, is the antithesis of the modern, the smooth, the factory-made—and hence desirable.

The use of either neutral shades or the more vibrant contrast of solid colors demands both subtlety and restraint. The reason is that, without patterns, colors and textures become more important, and unlike what happens with patterns, designers have not thought out beforehand how to mix them. Take the neutral palette first—not, of course, that neutrals are always so indeterminate that they sink into the background (think of the pairing of black and white, for example). But imagine the rarified combinations of string, bone, and stone: use them in textured wool or cashmere, as throws, cushions and curtains, and you have a look, urban and sybaritic, that adds luxury to comfort. Put those same off-white shades into cotton and create echoes of the scraped-bone colors of the beach house, the suggestion of seafood picnics on the sand and long summer nights on the veranda. In silk, the same shades will say exactly the opposite, especially if you change the textures from slub and loose-weave fabrics to satin, matt silks and bias-cut glamour. In silk, the off-whites scream Syrie Maugham, the extravagant and luxurious 1930s.

ABOVE Choosing a neutral color scheme gives you the opportunity to experiment with textures, as in this comfortable but unassuming guest bedroom. A Durham quilt contrasts with a waffle coverlet; taupe blankets catch the color of the matting. The whole effect is restrained and utterly simple.

LEFT A series of natural colors in beige and cream are teamed together for this autumnal group. The interest lies in the varied textures, from herringbone to nubbly weaves, as much as the colors.

It was not until the 20th century that the understated virtues of neutral shades became stylish. This was because fashion, whether in clothes or furnishings, tends to veer to the most expensive objects available. Before the invention of aniline dyes in the 19th century, it was a long and tedious process to color fabrics; this was true even of monochromes such as toile de Jouy. And, before the invention of powered looms and Jacquard weaving, most patterned fabrics had to be handwoven. As a result, the cheapest— and least sought after—fabrics were the plain weaves of a single color.

Fashion also reacts to what has gone before. When multicolored chintz and woven paisley were available to the middle classes, the smart folk started looking toward neutrals, especially pale-colored ones that were expensive to clean and maintain. This was why Syrie Maugham hit the spot when the generation that followed World War I reacted to the grotesque overstuffing and overfurnishing that saw out the 19th century and the extravagance of the Edwardian era that followed it.

Our current longing for the the neutral and the natural is a similar reaction against the vulgarity of the 1980s and the way the world is being taken over by industrial processes. We long for handwoven fabrics with

visible faults, for yarn colored with vegetable dyes, and for a lack of pattern compensated by an interest in texture. Neutrals are far from easy to get right. Look at the trade cards issued by paint firms and you will see the huge variations to be found in cream and beige alone. While any cream looks good with any white or black, few creams will look good together.

LEFT Clever mixing of different kinds of leather enhances the effects of each. Here plain dark suede is contrasted with brown overstitched suede and the softest glove leather. The colors are all shades of taupe and brown.
ABOVE No easy chair is easier on the eye—and the buns—than a leather-upholstered club armchair. The more you sit in it, the better it gets. This stylish version has a matching tan suede pillow made of irregular patchwork.
RIGHT Slipcovers for the sofa and pouffe are a natural cotton; interest comes from the soft cashmere pillows and neutral, earthy throw.

It's a question of the quantity of red tones in the colors. The same applies to the middle tones of gray or beige, while even white and black, which would seem safe together, can have wide variations.

Texture adds a further complication in that the whorls and ribs, patterns and slubs will catch and hold the light and the reflections from the fabrics around them. Try putting a piece of creamy Donegal tweed alongside red felt, and you will appreciate how carefully neutrals need to be positioned.

The simplest solution is to start with a swatch board for all the possible fabrics, from curtains to cushions to rugs, and add to that the shades you plan for walls, ceiling, floor, and furniture. You can take advantage of the way light shades react to primary colors by actually encouraging the reflections of one on another while also subtly revealing the intricacies of plain white.

Combining neutrals also needs a good deal of skill because some mixtures—think coffee and cream—are utterly dated to the 1970s, although no doubt they will eventually enjoy a comeback. Yet coffee can currently be happily allied with black or terracotta, while cream is being teamed with whites and beiges. A neutral scheme is therefore difficult to achieve, but is highly adaptable when you get it right.

LEFT AND ABOVE Neutrals don't have to be boring. The sofa shown left is made welcoming in this gray-walled living room by being a touch pinker than the rest of the scheme. The warm tones of the wooden cabinets also make for friendliness. Cushions on the sofa opposite (shown above) bring together the room's grays and off-whites without shouting about their intention.

RIGHT Gray, like black and white, comes in all sorts of shades—bluer, pinker, browner. When you are matching fabrics to furniture, check that the shades complement each other. But don't bother to get an exact match.

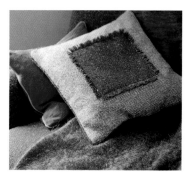

FAR LEFT Ribbon makes a decorative feature on two plain blankets. It is threaded through the loose mohair weave of the top one and used as a hem for the conventional wool version.

CENTER LEFT This is a clever way of using the charms of wool and tweed. The chair is covered in fuchsia Donegal tweed, which turns up as patchwork and piping on a pink herringbone pillow. The brilliant raspberry throw gives extra oomph.

NEAR LEFT Interest in green issues has led to a longing for natural colors and textures such as this roughly woven earth-colored blanket of wool.

BELOW Wool dyes well in shades of orange, beige, and brown, and this chair shows how harmoniously they mix. Herringbone tweeds are bordered in neutral shades and complemented by a tweed patchwork pillow.

wool and velvet

Of all the fabrics available to the 21st-century designer, wool and velvet come with the greatest weight of history. Fragments of woven wool have turned up in Babylonian graves; in the British House of Lords the Lord Chancellor sits on a sack of wool to remind his country that wool was responsible for its rise to power; and Renaissance paintings are heavy with the richness of silk velvet, cut into patterns that are still available in Italy today.

Wool is one of the most adaptable fabrics. Depending on the breed of sheep—or, I suppose, goat, llama, or alpaca—the textile that results can either be tough enough to be woven into a pile-free Scottish tweed carpet (a tradition recently revived by the Highland firm of Anta) or fine enough to be knitted into a baby's christening shawl that will, like silk, run through a wedding ring. Wool can be dyed in the brightest colors or left the original color of the fleece—anything from off-white to dusty gray or dark brown. Its weave can vary from the outbreaks of Donegal tweed, whose oatmealy texture is enlivened with random spots of primary colors, to the smoothest, sheeniest worsted made from 100 percent superfine wool.

Through the centuries wool has given the world classic fabrics: tweed and plaid from Scotland, now copied from Japan to Milan; paisleys from India, which arrived as cashmere shawls and became a Victorian craze that never went away; kilims from Persia, Afghanistan, and dozens of wandering Middle Eastern tribes that recently moved away from carpets to become hangings, cushions, covers for sofas and chairs, luggage, and even slippers. Flannels, worsted, and pinstripes covered generations of businesslike bodies and gangster shoulder pads before moving into curtains and beds, while knitted wool in all its traditional modes, from Fair Isle to Guernsey, is the inspiration behind dozens of fabric textures and patterns.

Its uses in rooms are just as various. Interior designers such as John Stefanides have taken updates of tattersalls (more traditionally found on racecourse-going vests) and tweeds to make fine sofa covers; the architect

THIS PAGE Tweeds were originally intended to blend with the mountains, and this lovely autumnal mix catches the flaring woods and brackens of Ireland, where all these woolens were woven. Being rugged by nature, tweeds will stand any amount of mixing and matching.

RIGHT An effective mingling of fabrics for a chair: the soft purple upholstery is made of velvet, while the generous pillow is silk with a more robust cotton trim.
OPPOSITE PAGE The room continues the effective mixture of textures and fabrics with a leather stool at its center, a large L-shaped sofa in neutral gray cotton, and subtle pillows in silk. The floor cushions are made of stronger cotton.

Sophie Hicks delights in using gray flannel to drape long Georgian windows in London houses; while Tessa Kennedy does outrageous things with multicolored plaid. The secret is to do the unexpected. A Fair Isle sweater could embrace a tubby chair; a blue chalk stripe would make a fine bedspread; and the discreet ribs of fishermen's jerseys just plead to be cushion covers. Harris tweed is so tough that it could cope with a troupe of performing circus dogs jumping on it, while the subtle checks and stripes of Scottish estate tweeds just ask to be mixed together as curtains, covers, cushions, and carpets.

Other European countries do use wool—I recently came across a thick teased weave made in the mountains of Tuscany to wrap around chilled shepherds in winter—but it is hard to think of any nation that has made such good use of its sheep as Britain. The Lord Chancellor's Woolsack is there by right.

If woven wool is a British triumph, then velvet must belong to the Italians. There are shops in Florence where the gorgeous complexities of 14th-century design, the curves and swirls, the cutting and shearing, the dyeing and weaving, can still be found, where velvet is made on ancient machines according to ancient secrets. Velvets, especially silk velvet, whose raised pile can be stroked like a cat's fur, were the aristocrats of the world of fabrics. Modern techniques may mean that their richness has been superseded by that of suede and cashmere, and their current unfashionableness has deprived most people of the chance to experience the glamour of a beautiful velvet, but decorators such as Alidad, whose Eastern roots enable him to appreciate velvet's allure, are slowly returning to its charms.

The aim should be to use velvet—or, for that matter, plaid or flannel—in unexpected ways and in unexpected colors. Velvet is, of course, solid-colored. Its variations come from self-colored patterns, cutting the pile to different lengths, or varying areas of pile with areas of plain, gleaming silk. The furry pile and the naked silk provide such a contrast of textures that there is no need for other shades or colors. The most extreme example of this is devoré, which made a comeback a few years ago, first as fashion wraps but latterly as throws. Here the silk pile is complemented by silk so fine that it is a

sheer chiffon; the idea is that, when draped and folded, the patterns should be endlessly repeated and refined through the transparent veils. But its uses are limited by its fragility. An uncut silk velvet can survive for generations; cut, the fabric becomes ever more delicate, though well-treated silk can survive where wool will not.

Once the cutting reaches its extremes, as in devoré, it will survive only as pure decoration. Use it as a throw on an unused chair, a drape over a chaise longue in a boudoir, or for the hangings of a four-poster bed. Consider cut velvet, too, as a background for a fine oil painting. The Old Masters knew what they were doing when they placed their Virgins and saints against backdrops of velvet, for its sheen attracts the light and, with it, attention. But, if your velvet is in the premier league, the picture must be, too.

LEFT Velvets, such as this operatic swagger of dark green, work well in nighttime rooms and in winter. In this room, they can simply be removed on sunnier days.

BELOW Silk is exceptionally good at taking dyes and, when made into velvet, elegantly catches textures and sheen. All these properties have been used for this tab-hung curtain.

OPPOSITE PAGE, LEFT The luxurious silk and velvet pillows in this understated room have been deliberately chosen to enhance the modern abstract painting.

OPPOSITE PAGE, ABOVE RIGHT Pillow covers don't need to be of a single fabric. Here silk and velvet are joined with a single line of piping.

OPPOSITE PAGE, BELOW RIGHT Velvet comes in all sorts of stylish patterns and textures. The top pillow on the pile is harlequin velvet with fancy tassels; the one below is velvet cut in a traditional damask pattern.

faux fur, suede, and leather

Real furs, such as the bear skins mounded up on the bed of Ivan the Terrible in old Hollywood movies, are clearly politically incorrect in modern interiors. Whether the animals they came from were trapped or farmed, pelts used in home furnishings are generally unacceptable to 21st-century humans. But we can't, it seems, do without the approximation of fur. We need the soft security of deep gray chinchilla for our bare feet to play in and the velvety texture of beaver to smooth in our laps. Nor can we relinquish the colors, the camouflage, the patterns that nature gave.

We now revel in faux furs, artfully teased from artificial fabrics and patterned as though the shy Polydamide once strolled across Africa's veldt, hiding itself from predators by evolving a synthetic fur striped and barred like strong sunlight against the trees. Even in its new, manmade mode, fur remains as exotic as when 20th-century design luminaries such as Diana Vreeland and Cecil Beaton, Valentino and Le Corbusier used real pelts, from leopard to pony, for their carpets, cushions, and chairs. Recently, designers of the suites of London's grandest hotels have upholstered chairs in mock zebra and bordered bedspreads with cheating cheetah—and the aura these rooms evoke is that of a banquet about to begin.

Pelts from exotic animals, hunted among the high deserts of Africa or the dripping forests of Sumatra, have been synonymous with forbidden luxury since the Romans lounged on couches bedecked with lion skins. Even though we have now substituted coal derivatives for the real thing, we have still not got rid of the baggage that goes with tawny stripes.

But this is luxury to be found for not much cost. The new faux furs perform much better than the old skins. They are easily worked by the upholsterer; they can be cleaned if you drop your lunch on them; they evoke no pain-filled animal deaths—and they don't suffer from moths. Better still, you can upholster a set of chairs, whether dining, office, or armchairs, in a mix of animals. One can be cheetah, another leopard, a third tiger, along with zebra, giraffe, or ocelot; because all take their colors from nature—a mixture of black, brown, fawn, and cream—they will complement each other, especially if you buy different fabrics from the same maker.

Don't confine your use of faux furs to upholstery. Suitably backed, the less hairy faux furs make great throws or even curtains. Real skins tended to be backed with plain felt, from black to scarlet, and this makes a good foil for fakes, too. Hairier fakes, such as bear, wolf, and monkey, work less well for pure upholstery—well, they won't work at all—but are fine in throws, scatter rugs, and cushions. Think Ivan the Terrible and pile them on your bed.

OPPOSITE PAGE, ABOVE Leather is best used to upholster versions of the club armchair. It can add an element of luxury which is either traditional or, as here, modernist in essence.

OPPOSITE PAGE, BELOW Leather does not have to be brown or black. New ways of coloring hides mean that soft neutrals can be used in upholstery.

BELOW Hide is one of the longest-lasting upholstery materials, which actually improves with wear. It is perfect for these kitchen stools since it can be easily wiped down.

TOP RIGHT Interiors have recently been inspired by chic luggage. These leather door handles are clearly influenced by Vuitton trunks.

CENTRE RIGHT One conspicuous disadvantage of leather is that it has a slithery feel. But the problem can be solved by allying it with textured velvet.

BOTTOM RIGHT Leather is increasingly being used for accessories—as in this practical storage hamper. Generally, it works best in natural colors.

In a glossy fashion magazine I recently saw a pair of fishing trousers: they were of the palest stone suede, beautifully tailored and costing around $1,500. Perfect for fishing, enthused the editor—as long as you didn't get a spot of damp on them. This is the point of suede: it is beautiful, comfortable, luxurious, expensive, and extremely impractical. And that is why we love it

more substantial. Used in the way Amberg favors—in darkish natural colors, severely cut into squares and rectangles and sewn together—its message is masculine. It somehow recalls the interiors of private jets and luxury cars, state rooms in 1930s transatlantic liners, and briefcases teamed with cashmere coats. Leather epitomizes the great age of travel and, used

LEFT An earthy brown suede pillow tops a pile of throws where both colors and textures have been carefully chosen.

RIGHT Even a tiny amount of suede or leather adds a touch of luxury. The plain cotton curtains are held back with a pair of soft brown suede and leather ties.

OPPOSITE PAGE, CLOCKWISE FROM TOP LEFT
A subtle mixture of textures characterizes this seat. The chair is suede with a ponyskin cushion at the back and a soft woolen throw over all.
A plain armchair has been closely covered in the palest suede to emphasize its strong outline.
This scheme makes use of realistic faux ponyskin for the easy chairs and places them formally on a fake fur rug.
A fake giraffe fabric has been used to cover everything on this X-stool, even the legs. It is placed at the bottom of a bed in similar colors.

around the house. Since the days of Jean Harlow, the palest matt skins have been used to cover beds, sofas, and cushions and, while advances in curing and protecting the skins have made suede a teeny bit more practical, no one could say that it was sensible to have it around young children, animals, or even those liable to spill their soft drink in a fit of absentmindedness.

While suede comes from the inside of the skin, leather comes from the outside, which makes it capable of coping with rather more; it has a shiny, slightly more impervious topside than the nap of suede, which sucks up liquids like blotting paper.

Leather has been making a serious comeback lately—not just for upholstery (where it has been used ever since upholstery was invented), but also for floors, walls, and furniture such as tables and consoles. A leading exponent in this area is Bill Amberg, who was first known for his handbags but then became more ambitious.

Leather was extensively used instead of wallpaper in 17th-century Europe. Most commonly originating in Spain, it was embossed, blind-stamped, and burnished to create the sort of baroque patterns that now turn up on damask. Since quite a lot of it is still around, leather obviously has lasting qualities. However, whereas suede around the house implies modernity, money, and even minimalism, leather stands for something

in the modern style, can evoke associations with first-class cabins and Pullman sleepers along with Art Deco curves and colors recently revived by Connolly, which provides leather for Rolls Royce's classier cars. You can also use it to reinvent 17th-century interiors, where it can perform the same service as tapestries or paneling: reducing drafts, adding insulation, and improving acoustics, while looking dourly decorative.

New techniques for curing hides seem to have brought both suede and leather down in price, and the sizes of skins available are, for some reason, more generous than before. This allows you to upholster fairly large areas without obtrusive seams. Do not be wooed into using leather in random pieces for patchwork. It is always obvious that crazy patchworking is a cheap solution that uses up the leftover bits from more important jobs.

Whatever you do with it, leather is a somber covering that will add weight to a room, while suede somehow suggests frivolity. If we were allowed to be sexist, we would admit that leather is masculine in tone and suede is feminine. And, I suppose, the most recent introduction into the plain, skinny choice—manmade fleece—is animal.

Manmade fleece has none of the problems of suede or leather. It can even be tossed into a washing machine when the kids drop pizza all over it. It is satisfyingly cuddlable—but, no, it will never have an aura of luxury.

checks, stripes, and geometrics

Checks and stripes have had a huge renaissance in the past few years, which means that they may soon become passé. If you don't care about fashion, take no notice of this—for they will surely come around again. If you do care, use checked and striped fabrics in new and unusual mixtures and colors to bring them back to life.

TOP Woven fabric makes up the chair back and seat, which is echoed by the striped rug on the floor and the checked pillows on the nearby sofa. The simplicity works for an office/living room.

ABOVE A bold gingham wall covering in red and white backs a brilliant yellow wall cabinet full of red and white pottery. It is surprisingly easy to match country reds and yellows.

RIGHT The 17th-century paneling of a Scandinavian living room is matched by the checks and stripes of the sofa's bolsters and slipcover and the chair cushion. Even the rug takes up the theme.

FAR RIGHT Nothing could be more out of date than traditional glass curtains. If you need to be screened from the road, consider the charms of checked voile.

ABOVE LEFT Star shapes are good fun, especially in a seaside setting, but they are difficult to make and stuff. Use a simple checked fabric.
ABOVE CENTER This cushion's dark green bobbled border is several tones deeper than the color of the stripes.
ABOVE RIGHT There are four different checks in this lively scheme, plus both blue and sage green. It works because, along with areas of solid color, each check has the same off-white background.
LEFT These striped café-style curtains have no gathering and are held up by tabs.

A few years ago, one of the best forecasters in the interior design world was asked what the next big thing in fabrics would be. "Checks," she snapped back without hesitation—and so it proved. You couldn't get away from checks, especially the simple gingham ones, generally in a single primary color and off-white. Houses were bedecked with red and white checks: curtains, tablecloths, upholstery, cushions, bedspreads, and even rugs were covered with little squares. Stripes in the same cottons and colors were running a close second.

Predictably, everything has changed. All-over gingham now looks as old-hat as Laura Ashley's tiny flowers or gigantic blowsy roses on English chintz. These basic patterns, however, never go away—they never have since the earliest weavers discovered how to create strips of different colors just by varying the warp and weft. If a gingham or plain stripe is rather boring—both are achieved by regular, all-square variations—stripes and checks are

OPPOSITE PAGE Linings in the 18th century were often patterned with checks and stripes, as exemplified in this French interior. The pretty floral stripe is used for both walls and sofa, while the red gingham—picking up on a color from the floral stripe—makes up undercurtains and other upholstery.

certainly not. To be inspired, I have only to think of the Regency stripe, in subtle or dramatic colors such as slate gray and dark purple, sage and black, or blue and turquoise. Add to this a lustrous fabric such as silk rep or matt and satin silks—and you have fabrics that are little short of palatial. Stripes can also be achieved by techniques such as teaming cut and uncut velvet in the same color. Stripes that vary in width and color, as in high-quality French ticking, soft Swedish stripes within stripes, and Ian Mankin's clever modern tickings all have a fine 18th-century look which, because it is essentially unfussy, suits modern interiors as well as older brownstones extremely well.

For some reason, stripes evoke the town and checks evoke the country. While there are silk checks to be had—ones that conjure up the black and white *Vogue* Regency look of the 1930s, as well as brilliant Thai silks and glowing reworks of traditional plaids—lush checks are relatively rare.

Checks in cotton or linen abound and, given plenty of bulk with a good lining and backing, form heavyweight curtains and upholstery good enough for a townhouse as well as a country cottage. The simplicity of the pattern means that they can also be adapted to suit modernist architecture—and even to satisfy minimalists who want curtains or shades to shield them from their neighbors and cut out the daylight. My own favorites in the check and stripe line are the handwoven French fabrics that were used in the 18th and 19th centuries to provide cheaper backs to pictorial toiles—each check in these is quite large, about 1½–2in (4–5cm) square, and in simple (but often unexpected) colors. If the fabric is genuinely old, the dyes will be made from vegetables, which gives an added softness to the already homespun weave from the handloom.

I have a fine Nîmes check (Nîmes was the origin of denim, a corruption of *de Nîmes*) in dark indigo and rose madder, and others of the same size that vary the rose or navy with a dull white. All three can, of course, be teamed together because the vegetable dyes are all roughly the same shade. Add to these the splendid French featherproof tickings—far more varied and convincing, and still to be found covering bolsters and mattresses in hotels all over France and even in train sleeping cars—and you have a rich source of country decor. I recently bought a length of cotton, woven in pale greige with a brilliant orange stripe at the edges, which I shall use to make bathroom curtains. It was originally intended for roller towels.

ABOVE A greige and off-white checked cotton is padded and stretched over the walls. The same fabric is used for the curtains, while the windowshade has a pretty lace trim.
RIGHT The closets in the bedroom have been given the same treatment as the walls, with the gingham fabric stretched over the doors and an ornamental dado below it.

THIS PAGE Subtle silk in neutral shades covers both the sofa and large stools in this serene living room—in which everything is subsidiary to the modern sculpture. The silks are all washable.

LEFT AND BELOW Shades of the 1950s are evident in this "contemporary" chair, which has been covered in figured wool. The same "cubist" pattern is repeated in the pillow, where the pattern has actually been stitched onto the cotton cover.

If you enjoy working with checks and stripes, antique shops specializing in textiles are a rich source of finds, particularly because the colors are often so unexpected. But modern colorists are working with heavy cottons woven in the East to produce fabrics in equally soft sage, pink, and terracotta—especially Ian Mankin, the tsar of ticking.

The advantage of new fabrics—apart from their relative cheapness and the fact that they recognize washing machines—is that the dyes used for different widths and variations of checks and stripes are the same. This means that, with skill, you can add a striped slipcover to an old chair, edge it with cord covered in the color of the stripe, and pile it high with pillows in all sorts of checks, but still in the same shade. Beware of being too clever: think how contrived a woman looks if her dress, shoes, bag, and brooch all match. It's fine to have terracotta covers and cushions as long as you add in the odd wild card such as a flowery chintz accent with minimal touches of terracotta among the pinks and greens.

Matching fabrics is one of the skills for which designers are paid. I recently toured every single suite in four of the grandest London hotels, where names such as John Stefanides, Nina Campbell, and Tessa Kennedy had been hired to give each apartment an air of luxurious individuality. Combinations such as tweeds with tattersall checks and Donegal slubs were used on the pillows and sofas and behind closet doors to provide a soothing softness which was none the less both luxurious and urban in its effect—a room to return to after a tiring day. Elsewhere, plaid silk had

been swathed over the coronas of double beds, and one of the shades had been picked up by an equally expensive lining, while the same plaid in woven wool might be contrasted with plainer checks and stripes of the same colors in the living room.

The point about checks and stripes is that you can bend them to your will. They make fewer statements than, say, brocade or a floral; they are more easily sewn than large and ornate patterns; and, unlike solids, they provide a helpful variation of shade and tone. My forecaster was right to pinpoint the coming craze, but the truth is that these plainest of all patterns have never gone away since weaving was invented.

OPPOSITE PAGE A Swedish-style room in Connecticut has bland chairs, walls, and a painted checkerboard floor. It has been given a lift by three brightly colored flowery cushions.

LEFT The fabric used to cover the cushions is cotton piped in lime green. The pattern has deliberately been overscaled to create a bold and dramatic effect that is well suited to a large room.

BELOW In the 18th century, dining chairs were put around the walls when not in use. Here three have been casually placed around a plain white table. The room's restrained decor is highly effective.

the new florals

Many of the new florals are actually old florals that had fallen out of fashion. These are the fabrics of the early 20th century: full of roses and fuchsias, ivy and geraniums printed in crisp colors on neutral grounds. Used in the modern idiom, they have a freshness that is appealing in both rural and urban schemes.

I used to get the feeling that every middle-class living room in England (not Britain) was covered in yards and yards of floral chintz. If this fashion had been spearheaded by anyone but an accountant, it was hard to think who. Each background was dirty white or mud in color and on it were flowers chosen for their hideous shapes and generally colored sludge brown and corset pink with luridly green leaves curling around the horrid blooms. Often the lady of the house had, over the years, sewn her own needlepoint for footstools and chairs in similar shades. (Except one aristocratic couple I came across: she did the exciting bits of dirty brown flower and lurid leaf; he, when not otherwise occupied at the House of Lords, was condemned to the slavery of the backgrounds.)

However, starting with the blessed John Fowler, good taste gradually appeared in these depressing living rooms. It has taken half a century, but now those ugly linen unions have been confined to the trash can of decor (though they will probably make a retro comeback in the near future). The designer Cath Kidston has already revived the prettier rosebud prints of the mid-20th century. They appear on laundry bags and padded coathangers, lampshades and filing boxes—and she wears them as dresses, combined with brown lisle-lookalike stockings.

RIGHT A traditional floral chintz is surprisingly at home in a modern scheme. While everything else is very 20th century, the fabric is 19th—chosen for its clean lines and unsullied use of color.

Fowler's chintzes, which look as stylish to the 21st-century eye as when he produced them in the 1950s, were very frequently reworked from 18th-century fabrics. Berkeley Sprig came from a wallpaper discovered behind old damask in London's fashionable Berkeley Square and, before that, had probably been inspired by a 17th-century embroidered quilt; the firm later adopted Berkeley Sprig as its logo. Ledbury came from the lining of a 19th-century German box. Passion Flower—a strong design that alternates flowers in urns on an ultramarine background with strawberries and hunting dogs—was inspired by a Regency fabric.

All modern floral designers search for such original documents—which are as likely to relate to 18th-century silk dresses as to upholstery fabrics. Laura Ashley notably found her miniature flower sprigs among the fabric swatches at the Victoria and Albert Museum, while Geoffrey Bennison

ABOVE Traditional floral patterns can, when overscaled, look totally modern. This pillow gives the room its only splash of color.
RIGHT Now that designers have caught on to the charms of 19th-century cottons, styles similar to this flowery chintz should be easy to find.

THIS PAGE The same floral, stripy fabric has been used for the cotton shade and the large bed pillow. Different fabrics in the same theme turn up in the quilt, the unusual chair, and even in a little storage basket. Sensibly, the curtains are plain white voile.

RIGHT A little bit of pretty fabric can go a long way in a simple bedroom. This floral coverlet barely covers the sheet, but that doesn't matter. Adding matching but real flowers nearby is a neat touch. **BELOW** Junk shops, flea markets, and yard sales can be excellent sources of undervalued linens. Look for hemstitched sheets, as shown here, and softly old-fashioned florals.

was so determined to replicate the antique feeling of his subfusc florals that he set many of them on a background of soft brown—a color achieved by dyeing white fabric with strong tea.

Today there is a more deliberate cross-fertilization between fashion and upholstery fabric than ever before. The lace, velvet, and devoré that mingled with the teensy roses and braided cardigans of *fin de siècle* fashions were originally more at home on tablecloths, tatted guest towels, and bedspreads than in the nightclub. Plaids jumped from kilts to carpets in the 19th century, but in this they were joined by floral chintz in the Italian designs of Etro and in Nina Campbell's and Tessa Kennedy's "faux" Scottish rooms. From the Indian chintzes that came to Britain via Marseilles in the 17th century—much to the delight of the wife of diarist Samuel Pepys—we rediscovered a love affair with the Provençal floral prints of Souleiado.

Where new florals differ from the old drawing-room drab is in their scale and coloring. Colefax and Fowler florals stand brightly on fresh white or figured backgrounds and are not afraid of using strong colors. Fowler also liked to change the scales of the early fabrics he discovered: a tiny print used in the 18th century as a drawer liner might reappear boldly oversized and sharpened in color. Other patterns might diminish until the overall look was little more than groupings of dots. As with all fabrics, the skill in working with florals lies in doing the unexpected. This is not easy, because the

unexpected is constantly being done—and becoming jaded in the process. Florals with plaid have more or less had their day, while the technique of treating flowers as botanic prints on strong, plain backgrounds needs to be carefully confined to a single use per room. The swags and ruches of the 1980s (originally dreamed up by John Fowler, who had been inspired by a bustled 19th-century ballgown) will probably not see the light of day again for decades, but before long there is certain to be a revival of floral prints teamed with strong but unusual solid colors, and flowers with leopard or tiger skin are here and now. There's plenty more mileage in teaming flowery fabrics with complementary checks and stripes and bringing together contrasting fabrics such as floral printed voile and gossamer-fine wool or tweed and linen.

The way to get it right is to follow the example of Fowler himself. The color board may be a hoary old tool in the decorator's workshop—but it's there because it works.

If your intention is to create a floral room that is reminiscent of the countryside and the rose garden, a floral fabric should be the dominant element in the furnishing scheme. So pick a juicy one, well designed and cleverly colored. Make it the background of your board and add to it the braids, the papers, the tweeds and lawns that you think will produce the effect you are trying to achieve.

For such details as piping on cushions, I find that it is always a good idea to pick one strong or dark shade—forest green, for instance—that is already in the material, along with a neutral color plus one other really pretty color from the original fabric. Don't be tempted to pick too many shades, however, or you will end up with an overall effect that is fragmentary or too clever by half. After a few days' contemplation, you will discover if you have made the right decision.

ABOVE LEFT A pretty floral fabric may have more uses than you think. Don't simply consign it to the cottage and the Victorian row house; put it in a modern kitchen or bathroom, for instance.
FAR LEFT Experiment with different combinations of fabrics. This pink print has nothing obviously in common with the multicolored floral, but they work together in a plain off-white room.
LEFT Only recently have we come to value old-fashioned florals for more than their nostalgic charm. They are enjoying a high fashion revival both in the home and on the clothes rack.

silk and damask

These fabrics are the aristocrats of the fabric world and correspondingly expensive. Used in quantity, they have enormous grandeur and must be carefully treated. In smaller amounts, the fabrics' ability to take dye will result in touches of brilliant color. Since damasks have monochrome patterns woven in, different designs in the same shade can be combined, as can similar patterns in different shades.

LEFT The sophistication of these chairs means that they could only be French. They are upholstered in similar, though not identical, damask patterns in different rich shades, while the heavy bullion fringe binds the colors together.
ABOVE RIGHT One of the rich autumnal colors used in this elegant silk-damask pillow appears in a deeper tone in the chair underneath. Such expensive fabrics don't break the bank when they are used for cushion covers only.
OPPOSITE PAGE A grand hotel living room—the home of the same French chairs—demonstrates how to mix and mingle silk damask's colors, patterns, and elegance with an unswervingly sure touch.

Without doubt, silks and damasks are the aristocrats of the fabric world. The Chinese invented the spinning of silk from the cocoon of the silkworm early in their history, while the word "damask" comes from the Syrian city of Damascus—and the self-patterned fabric probably arrived in western Europe as a result of the Crusades.

Despite its softness and fragility, silk is remarkably resistant—and does not suffer from moth. Thus a crimson Italian silk damask ordered by King William III in 1689 for a presence chamber in the palace at Hampton Court did not need to be replaced until 1923. Even then, the silk was accurately copied.

The method of weaving and the ornate patterns so typical of silk damask have also survived. National Trust houses in Britain and the great châteaux of France regularly replace their 17th- and 18th-century hangings—for this fabric has always been used as a wall covering as well as for fabric furnishings—and curtains with damasks that are woven in exactly the same way they were 500 years ago. Some specialized firms go as far as to use the old-fashioned vegetable dyes as well.

However grand, silk damasks have to be used with care. Their sumptuous looks can too easily turn into the kind of grandiose flock-wallpaper effect familiar from old-fashioned steak houses. Crimson is particularly difficult—and I suggest that you really need palatial surroundings and equivalent furniture and pictures before you risk it. The other colors are easier: ultramarine and midnight blue are grand, but more unexpected. (They

RIGHT In a damask fabric the pattern is merely hinted at in the weave. Damask is perfect for upholstery in grand but understated rooms.

FAR RIGHT Woven fabrics, such as this traditionally patterned curtain, can be left unlined because the pattern is visible, though reversed, from both sides and allows the light to pick up the complexities of the damask weave.

BELOW Although it has to compete with modern paintings and abstract lights, this antique upholstered chair is still the star of the set with its authentic 18th-century print fabric.

would look fine in the sort of Georgian houses found in British cities such as London, Bath, and Edinburgh and, of course, in Italian palazzi or the townhouses of Paris and New York.) Damask in soft khaki is even more adaptable, as are the off-whites.

Silk damasks work even better (and are just about affordable) when used in very small quantities. The decorator Emily Todhunter, a practical soul, has pioneered the idea of handkerchief-sized damasks, and other expensive textiles, patchworked onto pillow covers, while grander schemes use small rectanagles of fabrics to hang behind good-quality oil paintings. Such an effect can turn an average landscape into an Old Master. Teamed with tweed or plaid or silky stripes, the richness of damask adds stability and depth of color.

Silk—textured, intricately woven in herringbones or checks, left with bobbly slubs or striped in brilliant colors—provides a strong look in many urban schemes. (It is often too strong for the country except in a really grand interior.) The brilliance and constrasts of Thai silk are splendid for the kind of eclectic scheme often found in American city interiors, where it is ideal with Chinese porcelain, oriental rugs, and Japanese gold-backed screens; so are plain but textured silks.

I love the idea of a city scheme worked around a whole series of whites and off-whites with textures from satin smooth to near-chunky silk tweed. Try this in a loft or warehouse space. Let it add a touch of luxury to a minimalist apartment—and improve the harsh acoustics that minimalism often encourages.

Although silks were made all over Europe from the Renaissance on, they still retain their oriental roots except when, like traditional damasks, the patterns come from an entirely different tradition. Embroidered Chinese silk, with peonies and butterflies sewn on in satin stitch, the gold-laced fabrics covered with rank badges for ascending mandarins, and silk painted with scenes of tumbling children are still both easily available and relatively good value. Something a bit simpler would be more appropriate for curtains, but consider these colorful and busy fabrics for cushions, for hangings, for small bags—even displayed under glass in a tray or table.

But do keep away from crimson.

ABOVE Taupe, cerulean blue, and soft lime-green raw silk are sewn together for cushion and bolster covers on a large L-shaped sofa.
OPPOSITE PAGE, BOTTOM RIGHT Small touches, such as this pillow covered in a rich oriental-type brocade, can dictate the style of a room. In this case, East meets West.

pictorials and toiles

Of all the textiles used for decorating, the pictorials are by far the most fun. They include the toiles, from Jouy and other French factories (though illustrated cottons were just as fashionable in England in the latter half of the 18th century), the more robust chintzes that arrived from India in the 17th century, and some modern classics such as Timney and Fowler's designs culled from black and white illustrations—anything from caesars' heads to blue whales—exotic animals found on Andrew Martin's upholstery fabrics and the painted designs, using calligraphy and gilded damask swirls, created by textile innovators such as Caroline Quartermaine and Neil Bottle.

ABOVE LEFT Toile de Jouy patterns can be extremely robust and with a huge repeat. Take advantage of this by cutting out a single motif to use on a chair seat.
ABOVE RIGHT The same pattern reappears as the central motif for the headboard and for the quilt on the bed itself. The room's walls have a matching fabric stripe, while pillows and cushions incorporate a check in the same color.
OPPOSITE PAGE The French often use fabric instead of paper on the walls, especially when the room has a dado. This 18th-century authentic toile of Arcadian scenes is used for everything—but the room survives because of its plain dado and floor.

Pictorial designs are as old as decorating itself. Think of the huge tapestries used to help the acoustics and minimize the drafts in stone castles such as the Tower of London. Great expanses would be given over to the doings of the classical gods: rape and assassination, war and peace were all depicted in colors much more gaudy than they now seem. The bright yellows and reds have faded to give tapestries their distinctive bluish-green looks—but they are still a great way of making an old house cozier. At the tapestry

edges can be found charming details such as elephants and spouting fish, marvelous seashells on exotic beaches, and bouquets of pretty flowers. It is these afterthoughts that have come to dominate pictorial fabrics from the 18th-century toiles de Jouy onward.

A later toile, with a sidelong hurray at Napoleon's 1805 campaign in Egypt, restricted itself to pyramids and sphinxes without any symbols of victory, while others showed farmyard scenes, the complex dyeing of toile itself, and lovers in Arcadia. Toiles in the United States glorified the country's buildings. the lives of George Washington and Benjamin Franklin (accompanied by Liberty and Minerva, in grand old tapestry tradition), while English toiles from Manchester boasted of the empire, far-flung lands, and the quaint costumes of Wales and Scotland.

Victorian grandeur led to some absurdly printed fabrics with false swags, lace effects, and pseudo gilding—until William Morris and Art Nouveau designers created their own pictorial effects of birds in foliage, wreathed grapes, and vine leaves along with more obvious florals. These enjoyed a tremendous comeback in the 1960s, when old printing plates were dusted off and, all too often, scaled down or otherwise spoiled.

ABOVE In classical schemes the patterned fabric made the main curtain while the inner curtain consisted of a plain, checked or striped fabric. In this room the classical style is reversed to great effect. The chair is covered with the same chintz.

LEFT A complex pattern such as a toile de Jouy may need a border to delineate the curtain's shape—as shown in this example. Similarly, goblet pleats allow the fabric to speak for itself.

RIGHT The pretty toile de Jouy upholstery of an unpretentious tub chair is enlivened with a crimson tasseled border, which gives it extra pizazz.

OPPOSITE PAGE Monochrome schemes—especially in black and white—are very much of today. This one is extremely clever, with the curtain border matching the walls while the chair's pattern is entirely different.

RIGHT Old quilts are not always patchwork. English-made ones often used a single piece of fabric that was then quilted without regard for the pattern. The colors of this fine example are matched in the other furnishings.
BELOW A decorative blue toile de Jouy has been given a bobbly edge in contrasting red. The red shade is picked up in the striped chair and in the antique basket that sits on it.

From the end of the 19th century, decorating stopped being so jolly with, at best, the vorticist designs of the 1920s and 1930s and, at worst (if you like a good pictorial fabric) the all-white school of Syrie Maugham. But the last half of the 20th century was as exuberant as the 18th, starting with the unlikely fabrics and wallpapers of the 1950s that randomly spattered chianti bottles, red peppers, and other exotica on white-backed cotton or created gloopy-looking fish on transparent plastic for the bathroom.

In addition to the generally monochrome Timney and Fowler prints, which went from bed hangings and cushions onto T-shirts and silk jackets, Roger Saul at Mulberry went polychrome with nautical flags and heraldic devices, while outside influences were the ebullient wax-resist fabrics made for Southeast Asia and Africa. Those made for the East are less extreme and generally based on indigo and white or, possibly, a third color, while the African textiles praise their leaders to the skies with heroic portraits. There are also leaping dolphins, birds that turn into fish, be-finned 1950s gas-guzzlers, buses, and electric fans.

Despite their pictorial patterns, these fabrics are not hard to use. Since many patterns date back to the 17th and 18th centuries, they are excellent in rooms of those periods, as curtains, hangings, bed hangings, and throws. Since they are all cotton, they work both in town and country, villa and cottage. Some illustrations are extremely sophisticated, others are naive. You can put together curtains of different toile patterns if you stick roughly to the same period and limit your colors to, say, indigo and rose madder, or the charming tobacco with cobalt. The Java and African fabrics should be held by a common and predominant shade, usually indigo or strong brown. Around this can swirl as many yellows and reds as you wish. But keep Java away from Africa.

Chintz, too, mixes well if kept in period. Early patterns were basically Indian until Europe started to tinker with them. In southern France the Provençal pattern developed, while in Britain chintz evolved into classic florals. In the 18th century the craze for chinoiserie produced exotic mandarins, temples in lumpy landscapes, and Chinese motifs that are direct descendants of the hand-painted Chinese wallpaper still found in grand houses.

THE COMPONENTS

Cushions, curtains, and covers of all kinds represent the keynote elements of your chosen style and offer great opportunities for decorative flair and innovation.

window dressings

Scandinavian style, classical and pared to essentials, has recently redefined the use of sheer fabrics for windows. It was the interest in paintings of Scandinavian interiors of the 18th and early 19th centuries—where plain casement and sash windows are almost always simply curtained with acres of white and off-white voile—that sparked the return of simple hangings. Since then we have become more relaxed and rediscovered an interest in the Orient. Following fashion trends, curtains now have Eastern fabrics as borders, cutouts, or panels.

Some time in the 1980s—at roughly the same moment as the whole world discovered that there was more to interiors than matching the background of the curtains with the beige carpet –the whole world went mad for curtains. Where once a few yards of floral chintz had been adequate, it seemed at this period as though we were trying to double the profits of the fabric companies. The chosen textiles had to be not only sumptuous and expensive but also ruched, swathed, and folded as if there were no tomorrow—and they oozed over the floor like molten lava.

The excuse for all this showiness was that we were copying the authentic fashions of the 17th, 18th, and 19th centuries, reflecting a mood that the last gasps of the 20th century should be as unrestrained and extravagant as other *fin de siècle* periods. This theory did not wholly wash, however, because the style in question was derived from palaces or, at the very least, from grand European houses. We were trying to create the same effect in modest suburban houses. Frankly, it was not a good moment in the annals of taste.

Reaction set in, and the 1990s saw curtains that were lean and slim and intended to cover our windows and our decency rather than make a statement about our wealth. Early in that period, a Swedish writer, tackling one of those charming but spartan Scandinavian houses, described its curtains as "like Strindberg." I knew exactly what she meant.

ABOVE RIGHT AND OPPOSITE PAGE Simple fabrics can be given eccentric treatments. Here a burlap weave is shown to full advantage—the light from the window emphasizes its weave and fringed hems. From a foot below the window top, the curtain drops from wire clipped into metal eyes; more wire attaches it to the floor.

RIGHT Fashionable clothes have recently been given borders made from shiny, oriental floral fabrics. There is no reason why the same technique should not be used to strengthen and adorn the edges of curtains and shades. You will find that small fabric finds can go a long way when used like this.

BELOW In this unusual treatment for a curtain top, heavy plain silk has been stiffened and given strong metal eyelets. The eyelets have been designed to run smoothly along a thick metal rod.

curtains

Today's curtains eschew obvious extravagance. While the fabrics may be truly grand—antique 17th-century velvets, genuine old toiles, bleached and crumbling with age, French handwoven linens—they do not flounce like *grandes horizontales* on Parisian sofas. Their width is generous enough to avoid that stretched look of economy that students can't avoid, but there is nothing extra. Just enough of the hem lies on the floor to stop howling drafts blowing under the bottom of the curtains, and the lining and interlining are enough to provide warmth without excessive bulk.

Fabrics have calmed down as well. Where, ten years ago, there were gaudy striped silks lined with gaudy solids and braided with yet further complementary fabrics—not to mention rosettes, tassels, hanging silk ribbons, and the like—we now prefer our curtains to make less obvious statements.

In my opinion, fabric furnishings should never be allowed to become the main focus of a room. They represent the elements of the style you have chosen, but they should be subordinate to the pictures and the furniture. If you believe that you can ill afford to buy good (inexpensive) pictures and would prefer to spend money on grand curtains, think again. Good pictures are quite likely to be a cheaper option, and a better investment, and to provide more lasting pleasure.

However, the curtain fabric and the way the curtains are styled do emphasize the effect you are trying to achieve. Curtains represent the biggest area of fabric you are likely to have in a room, so cotton gingham in a primary color will immediately say country style; a French toile will hint at the 18th century; and a porridge-mix wool will tell everyone you are out of date, that you have not changed your curtains since the 1970s—or that you are daringly retro. Whatever you do, avoid flounces, and make your curtains rather modest and unassuming.

In a decade's time, the mood may have swung back to extravagance, so whenever you renew your curtains have a good look at what the decorators are doing and what swatches the best manufacturers are producing. If you are lucky enough to have limitless storage space, hang onto your discards. What goes around comes around, and if you keep old textiles long enough, they'll sell for a premium. I've never been able to throw

LEFT In reaction to the excesses of the 1980s, today's curtains do not ooze all over the floor—but these opalescent silk curtains have been given a heavy, exceptionally deep hem to drop them to floor level.

OPPOSITE PAGE, ABOVE RIGHT Grandeur doesn't come only with grand fabrics. This scheme uses a neutral check for the curtains, with complementary fabrics for the cushions and upholstery. Yet it has an air of refined luxury.

OPPOSITE PAGE, BELOW RIGHT A monochrome striped taffeta is used for these complex curtains (which actually have chintz inner curtains). Instead of pleats, they hang in bunches, while the sides are kept plain and straight.

LEFT A highly complex French striped fabric has been used for the walls, curtains, and cushions of this grand room. It works because the colors are subtle and soft, and because nothing else clashes with the pattern.

away a good design. At the moment my bottom drawers are full of Arts and Crafts designs—which are currently out of fashion—along with linen chintz.

Fortunately, we seem to have gotten over the collective obsession with giving our curtains linings, interlinings, underlinings, and superlinings. While it may be important for curtains, when drawn, to be heavy enough to make sure they do not billow out of the window, this can be achieved with lead weights carefully sited in the hems.

Personally, I like my curtains to have a touch of translucence so you can see their weave at night and at dawn in the first sun's rays. All that is needed to achieve this is a single cotton lining, preferably in a strong complementary color instead of dreary old beige.

ABOVE Some old patchwork quilts were made from worn-out men's shirts, and this red and white version could be one of these. If you pick a single color for quilt and curtains, it is possible to work with dozens of different types of check.

RIGHT The overscaled patterns used in the double curtains of this country room are far more interesting than a simple stripe and gingham would be.

OPPOSITE PAGE, LEFT A fine natural cotton with a heavy ruched top covers the window, while the heavier cotton curtain to the right has been used to divide off a small bathroom. The stool has a seat made from woven thrift-shop ties.

OPPOSITE PAGE, ABOVE RIGHT Tiny metal grippers along a metal rod hold linen hand towels used as plain half-curtains above wooden shutters. Such towels can be found in flea markets throughout Europe.

OPPOSITE PAGE, BELOW RIGHT In a flash of ingenuity, the owner has used striped and textured throws instead of curtains. The fringes at the ends are tied and hung on a metal rod.

valances Gone are the days when it was enough to get a strip of curtain fabric, gather it, and call it a valance. There are better ways to remove your curtain track (the main purpose of a valance), such as fabric loops or ties and hooks, so you may not need a valance at all. However, if you decide you do want one, you should have it made professionally. Even the simplest valance is hard to achieve without telltale unprofessional creases or tucks or faulty pattern matches. If you can't do it well, don't do it at all.

Alternatives to valances include small brass or iron grips, looped to run along brass curtain poles, that hold up the curtain fabric by pinching it at regular intervals. They originated in France and Italy, but can now be found in good curtain departments. The advantage is that you can hang anything this way, from an antique dishcloth to a priceless Chinese silk, and it will become a curtain; the disadvantage is that, with rough treatment, the fabric will break free from the grips and slither to the floor.

Victorian curtain rings work on the same principle but are sewn onto the fabric, which stops the slithering but can damage a precious antique textile. Other systems of hanging fabrics, such as square tabard tops to the curtains

that act as runners on a track, or fancy tied ribbons over the pole, were chic in the 1980s. If you are lucky enough to have a good decorator or curtain maker, consider a tailored valance—a straight screen for the track made in the same fabric as the curtain and stiffened from within. It can be perfectly straight or cut and bracketed in a way that harmonizes with the architecture of the room. It may also be quietly braided in a matching plain fabric or twisted cord.

How ornate you choose to be depends on the room. Bedrooms can absorb a few flounces. Dining rooms are often formal and a touch ornate, while living rooms should be carefully thought out because they are where you spend most of your time. Avoid any fanciness in a bathroom or a kitchen because flounces catch the grease and steam, and look tired in no time. In hot countries, they encourage snakes and scorpions, too.

OPPOSITE PAGE Although this valance draws its inspiration from the 18th century, it has a pared-down—yet grand—21st-century feel. The tassels and ornamental pleats make sure the the treatment is noticed, but there is not a ruch or a swag in sight.

ABOVE LEFT One of the 18th century's charmingly flowered cotton fabrics is used both for curtains and for the simple boxed valance above.

LEFT Chinese celadon green with soft creams forms the basis of this calm living room. Blue and white checks of different scales have been added to achieve an extra lift.

shades

Shades are a modern solution to blocking out windows at night or shielding an interior from strong sunlight. They offer the advantage of revealing any interesting architectural detail in the window frame while maximizing the light that comes in through the panes. A well-designed shade leaves the windowsill clear in a bathroom or gives a few inches of additional space to a small room.

Fashions in shades can be extreme, and a style that has lost its clout soon looks naff. Consider, for instance, the dreadful fate of the Austrian balloon shade. Where, 20 years ago, it was chic, now it is regarded as worse than any other window hanging—even the Venetian shade, which suffered the same demise a decade before. Simpler shades are less vulnerable to the whims of fashion. The pleated Roman shades—which pull up into a neat rectangle of fabric and let down into a similarly unadorned length of fabric—are still very acceptable,

especially if you pick a suitable style of fabric. This might be a good-looking, strong-colored solid (pale colors quickly show dirt in the folds) or a pictorial that can stand daily exposure without becoming boring. Indeed, if you are particularly fond of a pictorial fabric, a shade is often the best way to show it off.

A roll-up shade offers an equally good means of maximizing the light from a window. The rolled-up shade does not cover the panes at all, and when the shade is pulled down, the glass is concealed by a good-looking

ABOVE What could be simpler than this neutral Roman shade made of muslin? Yet not only does it cover the glass with the minimum of fuss, but it also allows the architecture to speak for itself. Such shades are excellent where space is limited.
LEFT Dramatic architecture demands dramatic treatment. Roll-up shades don't have to start at the top of a large window and end at the bottom—as this hard-edged modern room demonstrates. Plain white shades are the least assertive of window coverings. They are perfect for all minimalist interiors, for disguising ugly views and, in bedrooms, offering privacy.

THIS PAGE Office? Living room? Loft? The plain white shades in this simple modern room allow its purpose to be adapted at will from cool interior to room with a view.

OPPOSITE PAGE Shades do not have to be made from opaque fabrics. A fine white voile is left unlined in this Roman version, allowing a diffused light into the room.
BELOW Fine fabrics such as cotton voiles can be made more or less opaque by layering. Here there is both a shade and curtains of the same fabric.

LEFT Roman shades made from voile, as in this example, produce interesting shades and tones as the fabric is doubled and redoubled.

fabric—or even by a version of a scene or a painting that glows with the moonlight behind it. The problem with shades is that the mechanisms can be unreliable and need a professional to make them work well.

How many times has a roller refused to roll or gone up wonky? How often have you found that it won't quite complete its journey in either direction? Or, worse, that it snaps out of your hand and biffs you? Personally, I'd leave the bad-tempered things alone until someone invents a better mechanism (which may be centuries, because inventors are all so busy messing around on computers).

I'm not sure whether those half or full lengths of stretched cloth found in Italian homes and French bistros count as curtains or as shades, but—because they are not intended to draw and have no pleats—I shall treat them as shades. If you can find the ideal white linen or cotton embroidered fabric with cutout patterns, these shades are charming in bathrooms and kitchens and, if your room is overlooked, make an excellent alternative to glass curtains. They can also be washed with ease.

However, they don't look right in Britain or America on large windows and should be kept for smaller windows and glass doors only—otherwise, your house will resemble a French railroad cottage. An alternative is go back to the screens of the 18th and 19th centuries. These were made of oiled silk and often in colors as garish as the color of an oilcloth. They do look very strange—and bring a weird light into a room—but they are authentic.

If you need a shade at the window instead of a curtain, it is best to keep it simple. A plain white roll-up or Roman version will shield you very well and draw no attention to itself. If, then, you can add a pair of beautiful curtains that never need to be drawn (saving money on the fabric) you will have the best of both worlds.

sheers

Sheers were deeply unfashionable for decades because—I suppose—they were regarded as no different from the glass curtains that covered every window in suburbia, reducing light indoors while discouraging prying eyes. The theory was that, if you didn't live in the inner city or suburbia, if your neighbors never got near enough to pry, then you didn't need glass curtains. Otherwise, they were everywhere.

BELOW LEFT Fine cotton curtains do not keep out the light, but provide privacy in a country bedroom. The inner half-curtain remains drawn, while the floral outer one is casually tied.
BELOW White sheer fabrics can be used both to blot out an unwanted view and to enhance the bits worth seeing. Even in daylight, the effect will be light and cool.
OPPOSITE PAGE, CENTER LEFT Translucent fabrics let diffused light into rooms during the day, and when the sun shines, they pick up architectural patterns from the windows behind.

The Scandinavians have taught us to appreciate sheer fabrics that can block views from outside of our lighted rooms at night while allowing plenty of sunshine to flood in during the day. On warm and sunny days, open windows also allow the fabric to billow in the sun, giving a fine, fresh feeling. With their limited hours of daylight, northern Europeans know all about making the most of sun when it does appear.

Conversely, we have also been influenced in our love of voile, net, and gauze by the tropical and Mediterranean countries. A fashion for hanging mosquito nets over our insect-free beds led us to realize how charming unadorned, light-textured net could be as bed hangings. The brilliantly dyed voiles of India have also appeared as bed hangings, with color over color

RIGHT Self-patterned sheer curtains are good for large windows and help to accentuate the little balcony. The deep ruffle at the top has the effect of a valance.
BOTTOM LEFT Raid granny's linen closet for such exquisite needlework as this drawn threadwork half-curtain. The red crochet trim is an extra benefit.
BOTTOM RIGHT It seems obvious to convert pretty linen dishtowels into curtains for small windows. They have their own colored edging and wash like a dream.

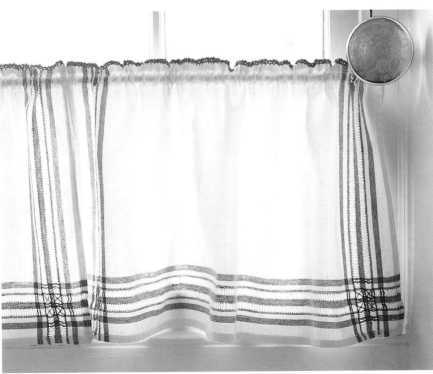

RIGHT Curtains can be used like screens to make temporary divisions in large or awkward rooms. This beautiful mixture of velvet and organza also hints at what is beyond.
BELOW Translucent voile is mounted as a screen to divide two rooms. It's an excellent way to borrow light from one to another.

creating rich mixtures of tone and shade. This is the hippy look, which first arrived on bead-strung dresses and kaftans in the 1970s and is certainly due for a revival.

From the Mediterranean we learned to love the simplicity of thin white cotton, hung without gathers at cottage windows. Teamed with casements painted in the evocative colors of Greece and Italy—an Ionian blue, a Tuscan terracotta—white fabric brings country charm while emphasizing the colors of the paintwork around it. Thin white cotton with age-old patterns cut in the fabric has been used as an alternative to net curtains in France and Italy. Strung on a brass rod, either at the top or halfway down the window, it is a far prettier solution for those

whose houses are next to a busy road. Take a tip from the Italians and use it to hide the contents of glass-front cabinets too. In a kitchen, living room, or bathroom, this simple cotton will hide multicolored clutter with charm—and it can be washed as easily as bed linen.

Sheer fabrics, by which I mean cotton in all its forms, are relatively cheap, drape well and are lightweight, even if used in bulk. (Don't even think about synthetics, which somehow look both unpleasantly shiny and dirty within minutes.) Swedish-style voile curtains, for example, should consist of masses of fabric so that, pulled together with curtain tape, they provide a good screen against the world. Voile hangings on beds can be simply draped over the posts, while doors, too, can be curtained with sheers that, on hot days, allow in cool breezes while providing privacy.

If your house is in a place where the summer and winter temperatures vary between extremes, it is worth thinking about using sheer hangings for summer only. As the fall arrives, these can be changed for heavier fabrics like wools, which provide a comforting warmth and won't billow in the breeze.

THIS PAGE This room is furnished entirely in neutral shades. The interest lies in the textures, from the fur rug and faux fur cover of the sofa to the softly uplit voile curtains.

slipcovers and upholstery

Slipcovers got a bad name in the 1930s and after, when most of them seem to have been made in exuberantly flowered chintz designed by a begonia specialist. The typical cover was made to resemble a large lady with a penchant for ruffles around her ankles. The early 20th-century covered sofa was a monster. By contrast, today's slipcover is almost indistinguishable from the upholstery beneath.

The modern slipcover is a neatly tailored job whose style is far less loose than that which characterized its 20th-century predecessors. Indeed, it may be difficult to tell the slipcover apart from the upholstery beneath it. Ruffles have become anathema. Either the sofa's feet are allowed to peep out from under it or the ruffle has given way to a neat edging—and blowsy chintzes have been consigned to fashion's wastebasket.

Today's fabrics for slipcovers are generally plain and neutral—which has the effect of reducing the apparent bulk of a sofa or chair—or they may be found in geometrics such as checks and stripes. If chintz is used, the design is likely to be one of the stricter versions, with flowers arranged in stripes or in such as way as to

LEFT This highly styled living room is characterized by neutral colors, but walls, curtains, and cushions are overprinted, seamed, embroidered, woven, and appliquéd to achieve a rich combination of textures.

BELOW LEFT When a room is full of interesting objects, the furniture can take second place, but this quietly upholstered sofa contributes to the modernist feel with its strong lines. The throw is equally quietly folded.

OPPOSITE PAGE, LEFT Leopard—even faux leopard—is in natural camouflage shades, and while the pattern in the room can be emphatic, it fits in well with old wooden flooring.

OPPOSITE PAGE, RIGHT Mattress ticking is tightly woven to keep the feathers from escaping, and it therefore makes an excellent upholstery fabric for chairs and sofas. Contrasting piping on this couch defines the soft stripe.

create a firm overall pattern. Sensibly, a great deal of contemporary furniture is sold separately from its final upholstery. You can buy it with a plain cream cambric cover, ready for the added slipcover that suits your room (and protects the furniture against accidental spillages and potential damage by the children or the dog). Alternatively, you can order the upholstery fabric from the manufacturer.

If I had the opportunity, I would always take the cambric and search elsewhere for a fabric that will give the furniture a stamp of individuality. After all, who wants visitors to recognize the same fabric that has appeared on hundreds of other sofas and chairs?

Added to that, I would be inclined to invest in two contrasting sets of slipcovers, one that is suitable for summer and one for winter. This offers the advantage that, while one set is being washed and rested, the other can be used on the furniture, giving a totally new, seasonal look to your room. Mind you, I haven't actually done this yet—but it's on my wish list.

sofas Sofas are for lounging on. Even such belles as Madame Recamier, in Jacques-Louis David's painting, and Pauline Borghese, sculpted nude by Canova, are convincingly relaxed as they lie on their day beds—and we should be, too. Of course, we would not be happy lazing around with the kids and the dog if we knew that beneath our seats and feet lay a fabric that cost a hundred dollars a yard, not to mention the hundreds more needed to reupholster it. Modern sofa makers have come up with the idea of selling their pieces covered simply in muslin, awaiting a proper cover—or, if the sofa is going to fulfill its perfect role, a slipcover.

Ideally, all sofas (unless upholstered in forgiving leather) need slipcovers. You can take off the slipcover for a party, to reveal the glory of the fabric underneath, but if you don't have a cover, you'll never enjoy your sofa.

Many slipcovers also have piping in complementary colors or, when the main fabric is patterned, one shade is picked out. Piping gives definition to the shape of the sofa—use it if you want the piece to stand out in a

BELOW LEFT A single spot of color in a neutral room is provided by a sofa covered in lush raspberry. The neutral theme of the rest of the design is picked up in the two pillows, which have bands of burlap as a detail. **BELOW** The strong lines of an upright sofa predominate in this scheme, though the upholstered base and bolsters are made from an exceptionally pretty cotton stitched with flowers. **OPPOSITE PAGE** Special auction-room buys of interesting old or expensive fabrics can be appliquéd onto plain pillows to give color and texture without incurring too much expense.

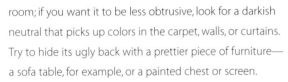

FAR LEFT Everything in this living room has been chosen to focus attention on the black and white photograph on the end wall. If you have an assertive picture, it is a sensible strategy to theme a room around it.

LEFT When a room already possesses a decorative feature such as this arched window with its pure blue stained-glass detail, why fuss it up? The owner has chosen all the fabrics in shades of cream and white with a single touch of blue on a pillow.

room; if you want it to be less obtrusive, look for a darkish neutral that picks up colors in the carpet, walls, or curtains. Try to hide its ugly back with a prettier piece of furniture—a sofa table, for example, or a painted chest or screen.

An alternative to the slipcover is a throw. One advantage of a throw is that, because it does not have to be tailored to fit, it is likely to be cheaper than a slipcover. A selection of throws allows you to change the mood of a room—pinstriped flannel for winter, for instance, changing to beaded African indigo for summer. Or you can change the throw according to circumstances. The dog may have its own washable blanket, but when friends come by, you can drape the sofa in cashmere or a paisley shawl.

Choose the throw with the whole room in mind: the colors should complement the rest of the decor, and the pattern should make it clear whether you want to emphasize the fabric or leave it unobtrusive. Neither

slipcover nor throw needs to be washable (though in a large family it helps), but it does need to be dry-cleanable. It should be made of a welcoming fabric; neither horsehair nor shiny silk is conducive to lounging, while corduroy, tweed, flannel, and linen are. And—while you may not want to encourage nudes to relax on the sofa in imitation of Manet's odalisque—the fabric you choose should at least be generous to uncovered arms, legs, and feet.

ABOVE Deep-buttoned sofas can be made less formal with plain upholstery and plenty of added checks and stripes.
OPPOSITE PAGE A raw-silk seat, deep-buttoned, adds comfort to a plain dark sofa, also in raw silk. The pillows are of tie-dyed cotton.

armchairs

Armchairs are a bit easier to deal with than sofas because they are smaller and less obtrusive in a room, but the same principles apply: easy chairs should be easy. As with sofas, I would use slipcovers to keep worry at bay, except in the case of those deep club chairs made of leather so sat-upon that it is as soft as velvet. The tailored cushions, often of brown velvet, should be covered, however—perhaps in a similar, but washable, corduroy.

Avoid the three-piece set. Have three pieces if you like—but don't have them *en suite*. While the armchairs and sofa may all be made to the same shape and pattern, make sure you cover the three differently. For example, the chairs might be in the multicolored stripe that is taking over from ticking—beige, stone, white, cobalt blue, and terracotta in varying widths—while the sofa is covered with a solid fabric in one of these shades or in a simpler version of the stripe. Add complementary solid and patterned throws for extra comfort and informality. This will give the room a less formal and bulky look.

A pair of armchairs, minus sofa, can be treated in the same way or, especially if they are not the same shape, covered with the same fabric so they don't look like random buys. You can also upholster armchairs in similar fabrics even if they are not in the same room. You may need to bring extra chairs into the living room when more people are at home, and it helps if they complement the chairs that are already there.

ABOVE The price of new armchairs, not to mention their style, puts them out of the contest. Old 1930s pieces can be found cheaply, restored and upholstered in your own fabric for far less.

ABOVE Modern curing techniques, which have made suede washable, mean that covering a chair with the palest hides need not be totally impractical.
RIGHT In this hard-edged scheme, the shiny texture of the glass-topped trestle table has been emphasized by the taut, shiny leather that covers the armchair.

ABOVE You can buy old chairs with comfortable lines and get a new cover to fit your scheme. If the fabric is pale, make sure it is washable and removable.

THIS PAGE A modern chair with an unusual swivel base has been covered in an unlikely deep-buttoned patterned cotton—but it works. One way to draw attention to interesting pieces of furniture is to cover them in fabrics which, at first, seem unsuitable.

RIGHT Walls of white silk have been padded in a bedroom to give the effect of paneling. The vertical lines make patterns in an otherwise plain room. **BELOW** Padded walls are an excellent way of softening acoustics and reducing noise from outside. The walls are silk and the hangings soft cotton.

In contrast with dust ruffles, headboards should be charming and decorative, and chosen cunningly to complement the bed itself. If a headboard is upholstered, the fabric should allude to, but not necessarily match, the bedspread or quilt—a check matched with a stripe perhaps, or chintz picking up a solid color. If it is your intention to pile cushions or pillows against the headboard, keep the board simple so it does not fight with the cushions or pillows but acts as a background against which to display them.

On a practical note, remember that headboards can get grubby and must therefore be designed for easy cleaning. Personally—because it is not easy to clean upholstered headboards—I would be inclined to stick with wood or metal bedheads (or fabric ones, if you must) and make mounds of pillows do the work instead.

The purpose of a headboard is not only to make the bed look decorative and furnished, but to create a comfortable backing for people who like to lounge or read in bed. Since we all go about this in different ways—slumping or bolt upright, veered to one side or another, or hardly visible above the bedclothes—a pile of throw pillows is far more adaptable. Cover them in fabrics that match or complement the rest of the bedroom and pile them up in front of the regular, white-covered pillows. Round bolsters and square French pillows make excellent stuffings.

Another idea is to make overstuffed pillows or cushions with ties and secure them to the head of the bed with bows. These, again, can be upholstered in the same fabrics as the curtains or comforter, but have the advantage of being easily removable for washing.

accessories

In addition to the grand productions of fabric furnishings—the sofas and the curtains, the quilts and hangings—there are quantities of fabric accessories in every house. They deserve equal consideration because getting these details wrong messes up the whole. Once you have decided on the overall feel of a room, you will know how to angle the details. The way to achieve a satisfactory result is to stick to the appropriate—shells by the sea, ferns in the sunroom, 18th-century Arcady in the Federal drawing room.

If you are aiming for an all-white, pared-down style of bedroom, your laundry bag on the door should not attract attention to itself, but you may be able to soften the whole with a tower of subtle silk boxes or a single Japanese screen on a wall or in a corner. An 18th-century living room would demand a different screen, in a toile or pictorial fabric; while frilly gingham lampshades will add charm to a cottage kitchen; and a tablecloth patterned with shells or guinea-fowl feathers will dress up a birdwatcher's hide or a gazebo. Accessories can be used to make slight modifications to a room. Suppose you have a basic blue and white chintz bedroom and you buy a

Japanese red lacquer tray—while not enough to make a statement, it indicates a direction you'd like to pursue. Add to the red of the tray a similar pair of bags hanging on the back of a door and an indigo kimono with red stripes on a hanger. Instantly, the room adopts an East/West axis.

If your sunroom is looking too greenhousy, give the lamps fabric shades of a white-background chintz decorated with ivy leaves or geranium flowers. Never neglect apparently insignificant details: white damask napkins in a formal dining room, old-fashioned knitted dishcloths by the sink, a series of boxes covered in a John Stefanides turquoise and white print of

LEFT The antique air of the damask undercloth on this upholstered table is emphasized by a white cotton sheet thrown over the top. The zigzag cutouts have an heraldic feel about them.

BELOW A cotton table cover is rigorously folded and hung to floor level to show off the wooden floor and bordered matching mats. The bright green grasses in terracotta pots and the baskets on the table hint at a scheme that is subtly oriental.

OPPOSITE PAGE, LEFT Robust striped mattress ticking covers a plain coathanger, and the whole is tied with darker ribbons.

OPPOSITE PAGE, RIGHT A length of plain ribbon, wound around a frame, creates a pretty lampshade. At the bottom, braid adds decoration. The lampshade is simple to make and gives you the flexibility to introduce a subtle splash of color to a room.

LEFT A small footstool is covered in dark velvet which has been imprinted with gold checks to suit its shape. The nearby sofa is covered in textured silk.
BELOW Fabric mounted to make elegant screens can be used to hide or divide a difficult room and, as here, be carefully lit for maximum interest.

dolphins behind the office desk and a matching fabric-covered pot for pencils by the telephone. You could even patronize one particular fabric designer and buy his or her designs to make your own accessories, from padded slippers and matching bathrobe to personal bound folders (a bookbinder will make them) for filing and squares to use as tray cloths and napkins. Those to watch include Cath Kidston, with her flowery evocations, Bennison's tea-stained florals, and Andrew Martin's jokey animals. Or take period fabrics to mix and match, such as toile de Jouy, French ticking, or William Morris's complex designs, which must surely be due for a revival.

OPPOSITE PAGE Patchwork was once the preserve of paupers using up scraps of fabric. Raid sample boxes and remnant tables to get this charming winter effect.
RIGHT This handsome tan leather basket holds towels and blankets in a bedroom. Leather is heavy, so don't buy big leather baskets to carry around.

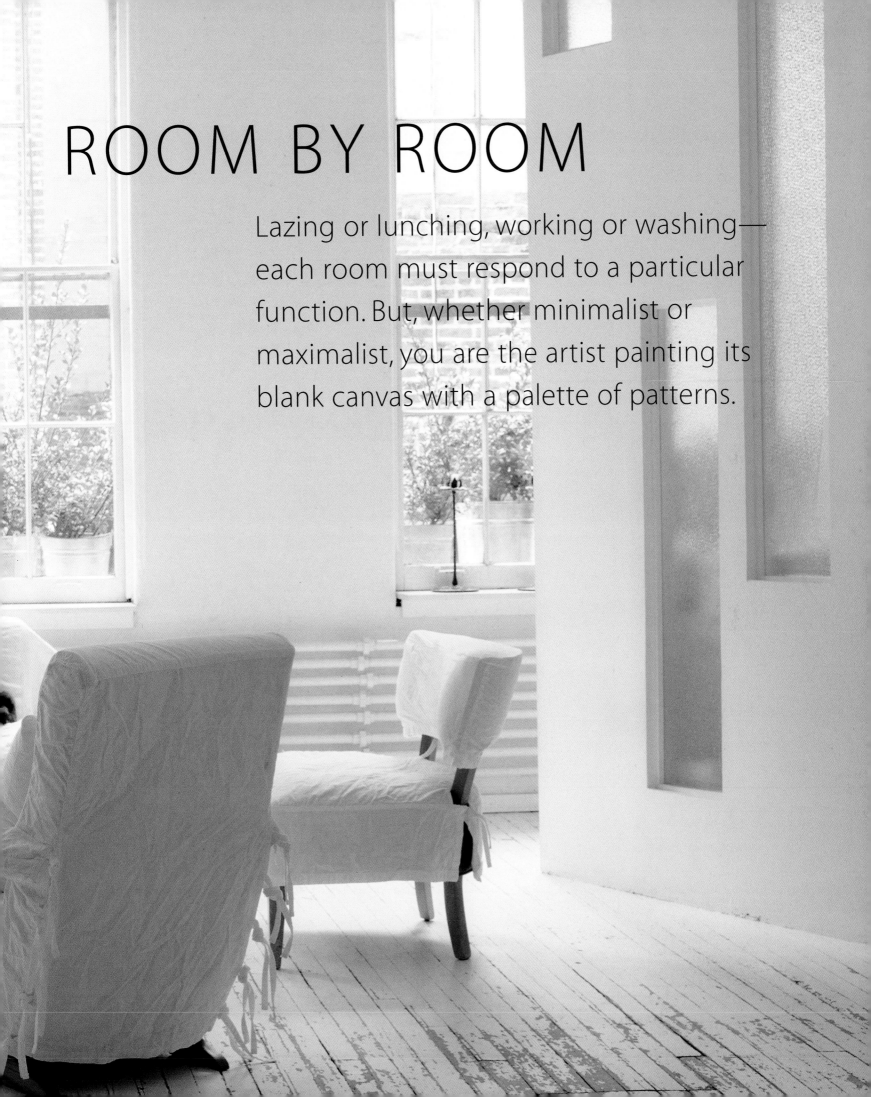

ROOM BY ROOM

Lazing or lunching, working or washing—
each room must respond to a particular
function. But, whether minimalist or
maximalist, you are the artist painting its
blank canvas with a palette of patterns.

living rooms

The living room is the most important room in the house from the point of view of design. This is where you and your friends will have the leisure and chance to appreciate how you live, what you enjoy, and what statements you wish to make about yourself. In the 18th century, drawing rooms were stiff and formal places where chairs were ranked back against the walls and moved into groupings when families and friends were visiting. There was no sense of relaxation about them. In the 19th century, organized groups of chairs and tables appeared—but so did the formal parlor, which was used only for grand affairs, such as a visit from the preacher.

As the 19th century progressed, living rooms became so cluttered—by chairs, tables with cloths, pictures, and vases stuffed with peacock feathers—that it became almost impossible to move in them. Drawing rooms and parlors were intended to boost a family's status by parading the best (as much of it as possible) that the owner could offer. The ostentation was designed to make it clear to which class the householder belonged and how much wealth he could boast.

As class has become less of an indicator of an individual's place in the world, style has taken its place, and living rooms are where style is paraded, even shown off. This is the room were we are most likely to make a statement about ourselves—what type of furniture and painting we like, our family values, and our conspicuous consumption. A further element in

OPPOSITE PAGE Two impressive modern abstracts are allowed to dominate this quietly luxurious day room because the dark carpet and taupe chairs with their cream throws lead the eye toward the pictures on the wall. So does the white pottery.
ABOVE LEFT Rich earthy suede on the day bed is echoed in the pillows and lamp base. The lampshade is made of silk to harmonize with the sheer curtains.
LEFT Padded cushions, neatly upholstered in dark suede, mean that this low table can be adapted into a stool.

LEFT Voile fabric behind an internal glass wall divides in half a severe New York living room. The softly colored sofas are covered in wool and given silken pillows.
RIGHT A completely different color scheme is used in the same room (see left) with its bright red chairs and flowery cotton pillows on a cotton-covered sofa.

the mix is that the world of fashion has been advancing steadily into the area of interior design to the extent that, by the end of the 1990s, the two had become inextricably linked. Think of the frequent shots in magazines of the newest interiors combined with models lounging on sofas in relaxing clothes (detailed in the captions along with the wallpaper and curtain fabric). The idea is to offer people a complete lifestyle in their living rooms, with rough linen curtains designed to mix and match with rough linen kimonos and drawstring slacks. Design firms such as Manuel Canovas and Monkwell, as well as fashion designers with "home" lines, are bringing out new collections once or twice a year, and we are supposed to adjust our rooms to follow these passing fashions.

My advice is to watch what is happening and adjust the minutiae but to take the whole with a large pinch of salt. Just as fashions return after a generation's gap, so do fabrics and the way we use them. Some of the most loved interiors are those where the owners have refused to change with changing fashion but kept the style that they personally liked. Among them are grand country houses where the original curtains, rugs, cushions, and hangings from the 18th and 19th centuries are still in place, Art

Nouveau interiors, such as that at the British National Trust's Wightwick Hall, near Wolverhampton, and Parisian salons where Art Deco still survives. These interiors are impossible to fake, and their value is beyond that of any fad or fashion.

If you are designing a living room from scratch, it is nevertheless a good idea to consider what's currently in, while bearing in mind that one day it will be out—and nothing looks less appealing than a highly unfashionable living room. Even if you turn your back on fashion and decide to go for a traditional room, remember that, after a while, you may change your mind. Design the space in such a way that the most expensive or basic elements will not date, while the accessories can be updated whenever you want or can afford it. These accessories are, of course, the fabric furnishings—which anyway have a life far shorter than furniture, fireplaces, or paintings.

However hard you try to avoid it, the fabrics and furnishings in your living room give clues about the kind of person you are. Are you traditional, with a liking for chintz and antiques, or authentic, searching out textiles that have been copied exactly from those of the 17th or 18th century? Are you minimal and neutral, surrounded by fabrics in colors such as chalk and string, or vibrantly

LEFT If you are fortunate enough to have parquet floors of good quality along with interesting paneling, it makes sense to give less emphasis to the upholstery. In this room, the sofa is low-key compared with the architecture.

BELOW Everything in this generous living room has been color coordinated— but so cleverly that it looks almost natural. Blond wood on the floors and in the tables emphasizes the amber shades of the upholstery. Even the logs match the whole.

LEFT The oriental feel of this living room derives not only from the objects and the table, but from the kimono-patterned mixture of pillows on the inviting window seat, which is itself upholstered in a slub Thai silk.

ethnic, with kilims on the walls and pashminas on the sofa? The answer is probably reflected in the clothes you wear: if you dress in classics, you will want a straightforward room; if you go for SoHo, it will be bright finds from antique markets and thrift stores; if you cannot live without a label, then you'll look at the home collections of Ralph Lauren, Nicole Farhi, and Donna Karan.

Comfort yourself with the thought that, if you had a completely clear mind, you would never manage to negotiate the vast quantities of fabrics and styles on offer. The proliferation of choice has been made worse by the onrush of communications. People travel the world looking for ethnic fabrics woven in the heart of Africa or dyed in the foothills of the Himalayas. Collections from all continents are piled high in swatch books in the major stores, and the auction houses increase their textile sales yearly. A firm in Nepal recently contacted me through the internet offering a selection of pashmina throws in more than 1,000 colors.

For a start, it makes sense not to go against a house's original architectural style. Although it is possible to transform a turn-of-the-century farmhouse into a traditional Japanese interior, not only will it take a great deal of effort (hiding the walls with translucent paper screens, covering the floors in tatami), but also it will seem ludicrous to anyone with a sense of place. So, if you have a Victorian artisan's cottage, copy the style of a Victorian artisan. This doesn't mean that you have to be totally authentic. You can use styles from the 1950s or the Art Deco 1920s, but it is crucial that the scale is right. Those "contemporary" fabrics with abstract shapes and primary colors that appeared after World War II are fine as long as the size of the pattern is in sympathy with the size of the window.

Today's fashionable loft and warehouse spaces demand something on a grand scale. You could try a large toile de Jouy pattern or an Indonesian batik in such an apartment, but don't skimp on the fabric. Curtains should hang from

RIGHT A country room with a modern twist concentrates on plain white shapes with only three red check pillows to add color and pattern. **OPPOSITE PAGE** A clever eye has used an Indian kilim to match the Native American fabrics of this Santa Fe room. Red is the only strong color that has been used.

LEFT People who collect interesting antiques, such as these birdhouses and cages, want their finds to stand out. In such a situation, you can subordinate the upholstery fabrics to the objects by picking colors in similar shades but a tone softer.

ABOVE Virtually every fabric in this room—from the kilim on the floor to the check shades—is different. Yet clever mixing and matching of neutrals and blue provides cohesion. A swatch board is the way to control the colors.

the top of the window to the floor and be impressively ebullient. I have seen one such loft space designed as though it were a drawing room in a stately home, and it worked well—as does the notion of setting up the whole as a Scottish hunting lodge with plaid curtains, carpet, and cushions piled high on vast sofas.

Richard Rogers and other top London architects have regularly taken 18th-century townhouses and transformed them into plain white interiors. Even the ornate cornices and stately fireplaces fit in well with plain white curtains, cushionless chairs, sofas in neutral cambric, and rugless wooden floors. Minimalism needs both discipline and the willingness to spend a lot of money on the few furnishings

on show. Those white curtains must be the best. Other designers have successfully made traditional English living rooms into celebrations of African or Chinese style by using the other countries' fabrics in a classical European way. A painted piece of Chinese silk turned into a curtain bridges the two cultures, while African textiles in stark shades—umber, terracotta, black, and ocher—can hang comfortably on a wall behind a plain European sofa.

Just as the way in which you tie a scarf can make you look smart or dated, so will the way you marshal your pillows and your throws. One year, a throw will lie in a heap, as though casually dropped on a chair; the next, it will be neatly folded over the chair's arm. Throw pillows divide and multiply: sometimes there are dozens piled high into fabric mountains; at other times they will be in a neat tower in subtle shades. Quilts appear in the living room before being exiled to the bedroom once again, while tables may be completely concealed by cloths that reach to the carpet or revealed with nothing but a small antique embroidered napkin under a plant pot. You don't have to follow these shifts slavishly—indeed, you should not—but you should be aware of them.

Similarly, watch out for shifts in color schemes. Living rooms may ask for bright contrasts—I always remember that of a famous art critic who mixed bright citrus walls with stunning scarlet curtains in his Yorkshire manor house—or they may lean toward the subfusc. The current passion is for subtle and natural earth colors, which can be found everywhere from beach houses to Manhattan penthouses. Shades achieved with vegetable dyes, always less abrasive than the chemical ones, are also popular, which explains the crossover of indigo from jeans to curtains, and the long reign of toiles in madder and ocher.

Consciously or subconsciously, we are following a politically green line. Earth tones seem natural, ecologically sound, and caring—yes, even in decor, politics plays a part. Another explanation for their popularity is that these colors are calm and soft and we find them relaxing after work. Also, these shades generally appear in the type of fabrics that ask to be snuggled into: velvet, fleece, rough wool, handwoven cotton, and cashmere, which are soft to the touch and drape luxuriously. Some of us imagine using our living rooms for long lazy weekends with friends—lounging on sofas in linen daytime pajamas and cashmere espadrilles, eating fusion food from Eastern ceramics and admiring a spiky modernist flower arrangement while snuggling under a pashmina throw.

Your dream may be different. The Dutch interiors of painters such as Vermeer may have made you lust after the heavy plain curtains that sweep the tiled floors of the Amsterdam houses, or you may see in the paintings of Matisse a carefree Mediterranean window decked with Stefanides curtains of Grecian blue framing a vase full of bright anemones. You may see yourself with feet balanced on a Victorian embroidered footstool in front of a bright coal fire, above which is a Berlin woolwork picture. Or you may want to display the kind of eclectic mix that is found in townhouses from San Francisco to Berlin, where every cover is tailored and disciplined, and where clever lights pick the glitter from a single Indian embroidery. If you can get in touch with your own fantasy, it will fuel your inner vision.

RIGHT A simple neutral check on chairs and sofas works well for a country living room. More checks are visible in the pillows, throws, and flat rug. **OPPOSITE PAGE** Stripes both on the cabriole-legged chair and Roman shades hold together a countrified living room in Connecticut. There are blues in the floral pillows, while plain lime-green versions on a white sofa draw attention to the profusion of flowers and plants.

bedrooms

**Unlike living rooms, bedrooms do not have to make statements
to anyone but ourselves. Bedrooms are all about relaxation,
comfort, feeling at ease with ourselves. They are, too, a launching
pad for the day at the office, for an evening out or a weekend away,
for a vacation or an imposing appearance at an important event.
They are the store and warehouse for all our clothes, shoes,
accessories, makeup, and personal belongings and,
quite often, linen closet and route to the bathroom.**

Bedrooms need to be highly organized behind the scenes.
The clothes, accessories, bed linen, and towels need to
be there, but not to be seen. The best bedrooms have a
guileless air of calm, space, and order. So, the first thing
to decide when decorating a bedroom is how to conceal
all these elements.

One option is to cover all the walls with closets and
cabinets—which will probably reduce the room's total
dimensions by about six feet. If you have the space, this
works well, especially if you can disguise some doors to
resemble paneling, print rooms (rooms with prints stuck on
the walls), or plain, papered walls, while giving others pretty
glazed doors like sash windows with, behind them, simple
ruched fabric to match or complement the bedroom
curtains. This will, in effect, split up the walls without adding
freestanding pieces of furniture to the room. I've seen this

ABOVE AND RIGHT Bedrooms are
growing increasingly formal—perhaps
because they are used as refuges
during the day as well as at night.
This dark-chocolate bedcover is made
of textured striped wool. The square
pillowcases are cream and bordered
in the same chocolate shade.
OPPOSITE PAGE, BELOW Curtains over
walls are a good way to disguise a small
room. Generously box-pleated fabric
in two neutral shades conceals this
bedroom's dimensions (and lets you
hide stuff behind them). Solid fabrics
also help to increase the sense of space.

RIGHT A soft putty headboard is made of ribbed cotton, while the bedspread is a softer shade of ironed linen. Square pillows and lampshade are lighter still.

idea succeed in stylish hotel suites where plain walls in Swedish green, rose-madder pink, and Mediterranean blue are broken up by green gingham curtains, bed hangings, and curtained glass-fronted cabinets, by blue toile de Jouy, or by a stylish flower or chinoiserie patterns in green and pink. Modernist rooms can repeat the same trick using a fabric version of the solid color that is inevitably on the walls. Try, for instance, white slub silk behind closet doors to change the texture of a white wall, or use near-black navy worsted behind glass and for the curtains.

The skill in a bedroom is to achieve a stylish relaxed atmosphere without overdoing the flounces. Modern interiors are especially averse to matching dust ruffles, curtains, bed hangings, scatter cushions, and padded

BELOW A welcoming London bedroom constrasts strongly figurative walls with a suede headboard and multiple patterned pillows. The trimmed bedcover is wool.
OPPOSITE PAGE Waffle-weave cotton is fairly easy to find, easy to wash, and cheap to buy. What more could you want in a bedspread? If you could bear to change this charming room, you could cut it down into towels, too.

coathangers. If you follow such a route, you risk looking out of place in your own bedroom unless you wear matching colors at all times. Avoid matching curtains with wallpaper—it makes a room seem curiously insubstantial, as though the walls were only as thick as the curtains.

When planning how to control the flounce factor, think about how you use your bedroom. Are you like Lady Diana Cooper, who stayed in bed until noon, dictating to her secretary, opening her mail, stroking her little dog, and taking the first social engagements of the day from under her pristine quilt? Do you, more prosaically, watch television during the day and evening while reclining on

your bed rather than on a sofa in the living room? Do you like to make your bedroom a haven from the family—or, for that matter, from real life?

If any of these is the case, plenty of pillows around the bed is an excellent idea, as is a washable bedcover. When you want to lounge around during the day, a bedspread will give the room a slightly more formal look than rumpled sheets, and you can prop yourself up on a selection of laundered pillows. Add to this a fire—probably the coal-and-gas-effect sort, unless you want to struggle upstairs with buckets of coal—and pretty tub chairs with slipcovers beside it, and you have your own boudoir or

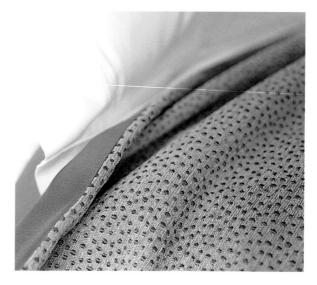

FAR LEFT The rippling pattern of the opalescent voile curtains is reflected in the circular moon mirror in a quiet bedroom. The textured silk bedcover has horizontal seam detailing.

FAR LEFT BELOW Plain white bedrooms are always cool and calm: a space to relax in at the end of the day. They also allow you to mix and match the colors of your clothes or to create patterns from them.

OPPOSITE PAGE, ABOVE RIGHT Small abstract prints make excellent bedcovers in modern or minimalist bedrooms. This cotton version provides texture as well as color.

OPPOSITE PAGE, BELOW RIGHT The overscaled headboard of this bed is covered in soft suede, while the oriental table at its base has upholstered, darker leather cushions. These colors are picked up by the three colors of bed linen used.

BELOW This soothing bedroom with its wall of windows is in a converted Scottish movie theater. The 17th-century oak chair has been emphasized by the complete self-effacement of the voile curtains and the white bed linen.

RIGHT In keeping with the rough wood and unplastered brick of a barn conversion, the fabrics on the bed are rough in texture and plain in color.

private living room. I don't exclude men from wanting their own private bedrooms—everyone needs to relax in private—but a male bedroom should exclude even a single flounce. One smart designer I know had to make do with a single room when he started out. Apart from being immaculately neat, he made special fabric boxes to slide under the high bed and created green baize screens ornamented with architectural prints to hide his clothes and office work. He went as far as having a large round table with a green baize tablecloth reaching down to the floor, and on this were magazines, books, and a central large orchid. It was stunning.

Indeed, where space is limited, solid fabrics work wonders if complemented by walls of a slightly darker shade. All the color can be concentrated in solid fabrics—curtains, cushions, screens, pillows—while leaving ornaments to stay monochrome black and white. Fabrics such as baize and felt can be stapled to the walls, both to provide a depth of color and to improve the acoustics. On the cloth, you can staple or pin black and white prints in formal groups.

When you turn from urban bedrooms, which generally look inward on themselves unless there's a particularly attractive roofscape, to country rooms, include the view in the general scheme. It was in the 18th century that designers realized that not only should all rooms look out on fine landscapes, but also that the landscape could be changed to suit the view from the window.

To create the best view possible, consider the bedroom window as part of the scenery. This means that your curtains should be at one with what is outside. This doesn't have to mean a floral or foliage pattern, but the colors should lead the eye on. Black, for example, would be a sad choice because its effect would be to intrude on the view beyond and block it off, while exuberant scarlet or yellow also impose themselves rather than leading the eye on. Blues of all shades match the sky, greens recede toward the leaves and grass, while white, especially in a lightweight fabric, is both neutral and encouraging for the sunlight. If, in winter, this pastoral idyll usually turns into a glimpse of gales and snow, consider adding heavy, dark curtains to cut your bedroom off from the elements and add a sense of warm security.

If you are lucky—or clever—enough to have a four-poster in the bedroom, make the most of it. The bed will always be the room's focal point, so it is worth spending time and money to get the hangings right. If you

ABOVE Very simple schemes in a bedroom allow you to adapt to changes in fashion both of decor and of clothes (which are an important element of any bedroom). Here the Chinese slippers are very much part of the design.
LEFT Family photographs make up the pattern in this modern print-room bedroom, but the color comes from a single note of brilliant aquamarine. You can often achieve the best results by being bold.
OPPOSITE PAGE Fashion-conscious folk might like to leave the color in the bedroom to the clothes they wear. All-white fabrics and duck-egg wall in this room allow the clothes to keep the upper hand.

can't afford to spend hundreds on just the right fabric, it is possible to economize by making the bed's linings, headboard, and tailored top in a solid fabric that picks out a single color of the expensive fabric used for the outer curtains and hangings around the top frame. In the 18th century, people were extremely clever at finding linings with tiny patterns to complement the important fabric, and some decorators or textile firms with their own collections still make unobtrusive all-over patterns to use

purely as linings. These little charmers can also turn up on the bed's pile of pillows, on the linings of the curtains, and behind glass doors. Even the laundry bags can match because the advantage of the tiny all-over design is that it is the most modest of textiles.

Country bedrooms can also absorb more clutter than those in the town. I'm keen, here, on piles of fabric boxes, from those large enough to take extra pillows and blankets to small boxes for jewelry, makeup, linen handkerchiefs, and extra buttons. It's smart if these boxes pick up references to other fabrics used in the room, but smarter still if you can vary the patterns slightly so some boxes match the curtains, others match its lining, some are a single plain shade, and others a stripe. Stick with high-quality wooden coathangers, all exactly the same. Although this sounds pernickety, it makes it easier to organize your closet and will encourage you to color-code your clothes on the rod. Even if no one but you sees it, the knowledge of a well-planned closet will encourage neatness everywhere in the bedroom.

Bedrooms may be the hardest rooms to keep under control, but if you give plenty of thought to the fabrics, textures, and patterns right from the start, it will make neatness easy—even enjoyable. Once everything has its place—drawers, boxes, bags, and covers all just the right size; blankets, linen, pillow and duvet covers piled type by type on adequate shelves; and the bed and furniture positioned to catch the early sun or the perfect view— you will find that being there is such a pleasure that neatness becomes second nature.

ABOVE This charming country bedroom is virtually all red and white—but with striped, checked, pictorial, and toile materials all jostling for attention. Apart from a single touch of blue, the rest is in soothing neutrals.
RIGHT This traditional American look can be easily copied. A pretty quilt has its blue and white colors picked up by the pillows. An upright chair has been painted to harmonize.
OPPOSITE PAGE As an alternative to buying from a single designer, you can also find colors and fabrics to complement each other by buying from a single country market. These stripes, checks, and traditional patterns came from the market in Tangier.

kitchens and dining rooms

I keep reading that the dining room is dead. Not for me, it isn't. While I do eat in other rooms, the dining room is the one I like best. It's here that proper meals are eaten, the room which is best set up for making the most of food. At the same time, I am starting to think that using the kitchen for meals is the last thing I want to do—almost as bad as eating in an office, relaxing in a room that is really intended for work.

The place where you normally eat should be as much defined as the place where you work, bathe, or read. We don't expect offices, bathrooms, and libraries suddenly to change into cozy, candlelit areas—nor should we expect kitchens suddenly to become conducive to eating or, for that matter, dining rooms to be suitable for cooking. Even if the two, because of circumstances, have to be in the same space, they should be clearly delineated.

From the fabric-furnishing point of view, kitchens are a near-disaster area. Assuming that you actually cook in your kitchen rather than just open boxes there, curtains, shades, pillows, and floor coverings are likely to become infiltrated with grease, steam, and unhappy cooking smells. I don't think it is advisable to keep any fabrics in the vicinity of the burners and oven other than oven gloves, aprons, dishtowels, and dishcloths, unless you are willing to wash them every week.

LEFT What other curtains could there possibly be in this rustic room but gingham? However unimportant in the whole scheme, every element absolutely must chime in with the rest.
ABOVE Linen, today a luxury fabric, is notable for its creasing, which gives added texture. Here a crumpled plain cloth hides the sink.

LEFT In a room as apparently basic as this French kitchen, the storage shelves are screened with neutral burlap, which is heavy enough to hang in perfect gathers. Simple fabric curtains used to hide kitchen paraphernalia are ideal in country kitchens where the family also eats. Materials soften the acoustics and make a working room more friendly.

BELOW Why have expensive built-in doors in your kitchen when a pretty gathered check curtain will hide the stuff just as well? But make sure the curtains are always perfectly clean.

ABOVE Perfect decorative touches make the difference between a room that looks acceptable and one that is stunning in its impact. The small strip of red and white gingham edging the inset shelf—and chosen to match the dishtowel beneath—is a simple example of how it can be done.

RIGHT The simple linen tablecloth is striking for its sharply pressed creases. **BELOW RIGHT** Overscaled checks upholster the 18th-century chairs, while the chaise longue has a similarly colored ticking to match the color of the paneled walls. **OPPOSITE PAGE** Lots of checks and stripes always create an informal effect, even in this room with its paneling and colonial chandelier.

However, it is quite possible, in the sort of large basement sometimes found in townhouses or the generous rooms of farmhouse kitchens, to divide the two areas successfully and, with the aid of room dividers and hoods over the stove, to keep cooking smells confined to a small area around where the real work is being done. So, while the kitchen end of a room may be a fabric-free zone, the dining area can still sport heavy curtains, chair covers, and the most stylish of table linen.

Whether they are part of the kitchen or separate rooms, dining rooms need an element of formality. That is not to say that ancestors have to frown down on everyone or that the curtains should be figured velvet, but that fabrics should not take the emphasis away from the food. Dining rooms should make food look its best and be an aid to the digestion. Restaurants are an excellent source of inspiration. A good restaurant usually provides newly laundered, high-quality table linen. This may simply be napkins, with the table top made of wood, zinc, or cleverly colored synthetics, or the table may be covered with a simply colored damask tablecloth. It, and the napkins, absolutely must be freshly laundered. No creases, no crumbs, no stains, no spills. Personally, I like both to be pure white, but I'm not dogmatic about this.

Restaurants also take great care to create a decorative style in their dining rooms that works both during the day and at night. This is not easy, but the colors, texture, and weight of the curtains should be chosen to look good when either drawn apart or closed. Cushions on upright chairs also need to chime with the curtains and be intended to look comfortable but not obtrusive. And, while every dining-room chair should be squashy enough to last a full evening, it is just as important to make sure that people are at the right height to feel comfortable

when eating at the table. Dining tables vary considerably in height, which can be disconcerting to guests.

Cushions should be anchored to the chairs so they cannot slip off while you are eating. Some dining chairs have drop-in seats which, happily, look formal while allowing even amateur upholsterers to change the cover of the seat as the decor changes. Country chairs are made with harder wooden seats, sometimes dished to give a touch more comfort. Frankly, they need the addition of a squashy cushion if your guests are to last the course. These can either be plonked on the chair, risking slipping off during the meal, or tied on around the chair back. If you choose the latter, make the tie as simple as possible—no room is helped by eight chairs with pussycat bows on their backs. Nor am I keen on case-covered chairs as flouncy as Victorian ladies in crinolines. If you want to buy cheap chairs and cover them, as they did in the 19th century, with cheap cotton cases, make them as simple and washable as you can, but this option may cost more than buying nice chairs in the first place.

Dining tables of any quality cost as much as a small car, and few people want to splash out to this extent. The answer is, therefore, to find or to make a generously sized

table from plywood or composite board and cover it with a pretty cloth. If the legs are good, make sure they stay visible; if they are simple trestles, cover the table at all times with the kind of moquette or chenille heavy cloth used by the Victorians. At meal times, add a plain white tablecloth or pretty cotton chosen to suit the permanent undercloth.

Few people bother any more with tablecloths, napkins, or traycloths, so there are lots of beauties to be discovered in antique shops. Look for top-quality damask napkins and tablecloths, or find lovingly embroidered sets done by Great Aunt Emily and thrown out by her ungrateful family. For the undercloth, search for paisley shawls that have worn out in the center, thin kilims, and oriental rugs (used for tablecloths in Tudor times) and fine silk curtains; since these undercloths will be protected by the real tablecloths, they will rarely need cleaning. Even a quilt looks splendid in this context.

If you are nervous that the dining area of the room will absorb cooking smells from the nearby kitchen, copy the clever idea devised by *World of Interiors*. Over a decade ago, a stylist found a factory that made linen dishtowels that have a 2-inch-wide red or blue stripe with the words "Made in Ireland" and "Glass Cloth" woven into it. She ordered many yards of the stuff and used it to make pillow covers, napkins, tablecloths, and

ABOVE The dark wood of this stylish dining chair has been softened by a pale upholstered cover that is echoed by the tablecloths. The chair's quasi-oriental design is emphasized by the use of a Japanese flower arrangement and Chinese dim-sum boxes.
RIGHT AND FAR RIGHT This dining room exemplifies how a good eye can create a sophisticated effect from inexpensive and disparate elements. Multicolored chair seats and tablecloths all have touches of grass green that are pointed up by the green dishes.

curtains. It looked both crisp and sophisticated and could be washed every week. Similarly, Roger Banks-Pye of Colefax—who was passionate about blue and white—bought a whole pile of matching blue and white checked table napkins and had them sewn up into curtains.

With some ingenuity, it is possible to find fabrics that actually enjoy being washed at least once a month, and even benefit from it. Think, for example, of blue denim, the printed African indigo batik that fades and softens with washing. and everything from ticking to dishcloths to floor cloths that are intended to soak up the dirt and enjoy it.

Both kitchens and dining rooms allow us plenty of license. Kitchens are working rooms that need no fluffing up. The equipment, recipe books, color ingredients, and plain metal pans provide all the color and excitement a room needs. Any cushions or curtains should be in keeping with the purpose of making good food. A dining room is more like a theatrical setting, designed for impact. Even modernist dining rooms can benefit from a study of how they were in the past. Fabric colors were chosen with candlelight in mind (even if it's now electricity on a dimmer switch) and the type and textures were those that reflected the glow and added to it. Textiles that improved the acoustics were always preferred, whether they were carpets, tapestries, or napped fabrics such as velvet or moquette.

If the style you have adopted in a dining area does not make you and your guests feel comfortable, by definition it's not stylish.

ABOVE LEFT The two-toned blue stripe upholstery of these chairs is made of short-pile velvet.
BELOW The chair seats are upholstered in cotton with a slight slub. Double piping shows attention to fine detail.

LEFT AND ABOVE Off-white fabrics are used for both curtains and chair covers for a Parisian monochrome setting. The wooden walls, chairs, table, and shelves are dark brown. The lampshades are silk and also off-white.
OPPOSITE PAGE Six stylish chairs in a classical Grecian style are covered with a broad horizontal stripe and set around a table that is totally covered in mouse-brown felt.

bathrooms

Giuseppe di Lampedusa's *The Leopard*, set in a Sicilian palazzo, first made me want a splendid bathroom; visits to Italy increased the longing. Luxuriously simple, Italian bathrooms have acres of marble—red, white, gray, or green—along with pure-white towels, bathmats, robes, and slippers. That is really all a bathroom needs—especially if the walk-in shower is the size of a small room and the bathtub is adequate for a medium-sized hippopotamus.

ABOVE Bright yellow cotton curtains not only give a bathroom privacy, but provide color in an otherwise all-white scheme.
OPPOSITE PAGE These bathroom curtains are sewn with tiny shells (a job for the long winter nights), while the choice of soft lavender for towels and robe brings out a similar shade in the opalescent glass.
RIGHT Not just a bathroom, this is a place to lounge, with a cotton-covered chair and footstool plus a gold leather chair by the sink.

Bathrooms should always look fresh. This means that they should have good-quality clean linen in carefully chosen colors, and the towels should come in all sizes for guests, because people are surprisingly fussy about the size of towel they prefer for any one job. Towels should always appear new. While it is tempting to carry on with a set whose middle has lost its nap and whose edges have frayed to tassels—don't. Bath towels, even in good cotton and linen, are pretty cheap unless you insist on designer ware. Drape a couple of towels over a rod and pile the others up in tempting heaps for later use.

Unless you have a bathroom fit for an Italian palazzo, the space will frequently get steamy, so make sure that more permanent fabrics can be regularly washed. Plain cotton curtains, perhaps with a waffle texture reminiscent

of towels, are probably the best bet, while shades are good (as long as they can be wiped) because they give you the opportunity to put attractive scent bottles and items of makeup on the windowsill.

If you have a large bathroom, you can have lots of fun. I especially like a bathroom with a rolltop tub in the center, which allows you to arrange the rest of the space like a charming living room. Cane furniture covered with pretty, easily laundered cushions is perfect for lounging, throwing clothes over, or relaxing in a huge towel after a bath. In this type of bathroom, allow yourself long chintz curtains that match the cushions along with inner swathes of white voile to give a charming country look. Bathrooms of this size can survive a few flounces, especially if the room has a view over the countryside. I am not in favor of too much fuss around the walls—no

ABOVE Shower and bath curtains are always a problem because of the constant moisture. A simple white fabric is used here—but decoratively tied when not in use.
LEFT A thoroughly inviting sofa at the foot of the bathtub breaks down the boundaries between living area and bathroom.
OPPOSITE PAGE Understated use of grand fabrics makes this bathroom the height of luxury. The blond curtains and cushions, detailed with matching braid, are deliberately the same shade as the soft carpet and the wood panels surrounding the bathtub.

floral-painted tiles, please, or tiles with gloopy fish or 1970s geometric patterns. The patterns should be left to the fabrics you use. This should start with a simple bathmat or two, always washable, to cover an uncarpeted floor (carpets are best avoided in the bathroom) and work up to accessories such as laundry bags. If you have several bathrooms in your house or apartment, it's a good idea to have the same color theme in all of them because this will reduce the number of towels and accessories you need and make regular washing much easier.

Many houses also have half-bathrooms intended for handwashing or use by guests rather than full-scale bathing. These need the same meticulous care, although they can be decorated with more daring. I know one collector who filled a downstairs half-baths with stuffed animals in glass cases and another who had letters written to him by famous people framed and hung on the walls—which goes to show that this sort of room can be themed. It is a place to hang jumble-sale buys such as guest towels with finely tatted edges and old school laundry bags; you can make it like a 1950s room with curtains with abstract shapes as decoration, or imagine that this is part of a school or Shaker lodging house, with institutional white tiles, huckaback towels, and curtains made from old dishtowels that mark a milestone. Beach-house bathrooms may be decked with shells, loofahs, pumice stones, and piles of sponges along with curtains patterned with sailing ships or seabirds' feathers. I have even seen a bathroom in open-plan style whose walls were made of tightly flexed blue-and-white-striped canvas.

While most bathrooms includes a toilet in the room, sometimes the two are separate. Even the tiniest can be given an element of fun—from curtains adorned with dinosaurs or prints of lions and tigers to zebra-skin floor rugs, chinoiserie cord pulls, or chintz fabrics whose ferny patterns match real fern houseplants.

Even in the smallest spaces, such amusing elements can be extended to tiny cabin bathrooms on yachts and in RVs or the rounded turrets of castles where the garderobe is traditionally situated. You can imitate the houses of the British Landmark Trust, whose bathrooms vary from a circular space inspired by a gothic tower to one that requires crossing an open roof in your bathrobe. Take time to choose appropriate details down to the last washcloth that matches the tooth glass and the soapdish in period and style. It's great fun to track down gothic-style fabrics to suit the arched windows, the basin and ewer, and the wooden towel rod found buried in a secondhand store.

So, while bathrooms should remain relatively austere in atmosphere, there is plenty of research and sourcing to be done to make the most of even the smallest, steamiest space.

BELOW In a minimalist bathroom, divided from a studio apartment, a touch of luxury comes with the hanging lantern. This is an area whose effect relies solely on shape and texture.

LEFT This bathroom, in a one-room home, is divided from the rest of the living area by soft voile curtains. Yet it is so decorative that it could well by displayed when not in use. **OPPOSITE PAGE AND ABOVE RIGHT** A gigantic towel horse is used to screen a rolltop bathtub with heavy white cotton. It will act as a shower curtain and draft excluder as well as softening a large, simple bathroom. No towel horse actually comes in this size, but it's easily made. Then it can be used not only to drape protective heavy cotton around the tub, but to hang a selection of colorful towels.

halls and landings

The main rooms of a house or apartment always get the most attention, but there are other spaces that need thought and imagination. If you live in a townhouse, whether in New York, London, Amsterdam, or Edinburgh, the vital link with each room and each floor is the staircase hall. If you have a larger property, it is the entrance hall that creates the first impression, and all those corner landings can be transformed into anything from a favorite sun-filled sitting place to a relaxed home office. Equally, attic rooms, spaces under the eaves, old pantries, and attached lean-tos can, with skill, be made into some of the most important rooms in the house.

While the large rooms in a house are there for the major events of the day, the smaller rooms add character and charm, and the staircase and hall are the areas that pull the whole thing together. People frequently forget that a house should be treated as a whole entity, with each decorative scheme being connected with the next—and the stairs are the place where that trick can be performed. On the whole, the decorative scheme of a hall, landing, or stairway should

be a lower-key version of what the rest of the decor is about. That is not to say it cannot be flamboyant—you can get away with stronger stripes, brighter colors and more theatrical effects in a hall than in a living room—but halls and stairways should encourage a sense of anticipation so that, when you reach the main rooms, you feel excited rather than let down. Halls and stairs should therefore be rather simple in their effect. They need few curtains, but those that are there should all be the same; the stair carpet should resemble that in an art gallery—classy but monotone—and any decorative flourishes should be saved for the rooms themselves.

In a tall townhouse, for instance, it is possible to have the carpet dark gray, the high windows curtained with black and white toile. and to signal changes in design by changing the type of pictures as each floor is reached. The hall may have black and white classical prints, while the walls bordering the stairs leading up to the next floor have great blocks of colored 18th-century prints, which in turn give way to modern abstracts. Thus, while the basic decorative scheme involves the minimum number of colors, you get a sense that the rooms leading off will be surprisingly varied.

More generous houses have more generous landings on each floor, and these can be turned into small havens of comfort and style. I remember a charming house I visited where one landing had a large bureau bookcase in front of heavy tapestry curtains. The chair beside the desk was upholstered in a pretty matching fabric, and the whole area was hung with large 18th-century prints of birds. This was the owner's office, where a large window looked

OPPOSITE PAGE, ABOVE Stairways and halls often need curtains to keep out drafts and to make sense of a scheme that involves walls, stairs, and windows. This elegant velvet curtain has appliquéd geometric patches to match the shape of the curtain heading.
OPPOSITE PAGE, BELOW LEFT AND RIGHT When decorating a hall, you don't need to bother about a source of light for reading or eating. Go for effect instead. These heavy curtains complement the wallpaper, chair cover, and carpet. A curtain detail shows how a floral border has been used to link the plain and floral elements of the scheme.
RIGHT A sunny sitting area has been created in an upstairs landing bay window. The blue and white checked cushions don't quite match the curtains—which makes the whole area more relaxed.

BELOW Deep-buttoned cushions pad this built-in Chippendale-style corner bench, while cream-striped pillows are bordered in black. In a monochrome scheme, the abstract pillow patterns are highly effective.

BELOW RIGHT Dark tan suede covers a padded cushion on a sunny window seat, and the same leather is used as a decorative trimming on the shade. The design on the pillows replicates a 17th-century embroidery.

out on the long backyard behind the house. It was beautifully decorated, strategically placed for visitors, and had one of the most attractive views in the whole building.

It is often the case that a small corner has the best morning sunlight or the most charming view in a house. Make the most of the space as a private breakfast room, a sunny place for a glass of wine at noon in winter, or a tiny sitting area to be kept for your exclusive use.

A landing or odd corner can be treated as a separate room with its own pretty curtains and cushions (which, because the area is bound to be small, can be exquisite). You can even mark the territory by using a color scheme for walls, floor, and fabrics that is different from, but allied to, the decorative scheme of the passage or stairway. You can also, in this sort of area, increase the comfort factor by adding more cushions, paintings, and rugs than would be normal in such a space.

OPPOSITE PAGE A choice of luscious fabrics in near-clashing reds and pinks transforms a potentially stark hallway into an exotic and inviting part of the house.

outdoors

Despite their unreliable climate, one of the keenest outdoor nations are the Swedes, who have thriving sidewalk cafés to greet the late sun and summer houses by the dozen around the lakes and inlets of Stockholm. Indeed, to achieve an exciting outdoor style, we might just as well take ideas from Scandinavia as from traditional Mediterranean outdoor rooms, where heavy grapevines and wisterias are planted to shade brilliantly blue-colored patios.

Outdoor rooms, and semi-outdoor spaces such as conservatories and garden rooms, should be considered as extra living and dining rooms. It is here that we can entertain large parties for lunch or supper under the stars; it's here that children most enjoy themselves, and where, on lazy weekends, we can sit all day, from brunch with the papers till midnight with a glass of wine.

So traditional teak outdoor furniture is not enough. It needs masses of pretty cushions, which can be kept in a dry storeroom in a willow basket ready to bring out when the sun shines. The slatted teak table looks prettier for dinner if it has an antique tablecloth under a fine array of glasses, silverware, and sharply folded napkins. You can change the mood in a trice and make an Italian lunch of black olives, salami, cheese, and bread on bright pottery casually set down on a plain bright linen cloth or one of those complex Provençal prints that at once recall the sun.

Garden rooms and conservatories are prime sites for squashy cushions on cane chairs. Here are places to use pretty chintzes adorned with simple patterns of fuchsias or geraniums of the type for which Colefax and Fowler are famous, or an evocative modern floral of rosebuds and carnations—sweetly old-fashioned designs imperceptibly modernized by a change of color and scale. If the garden room is by the ocean, use stripes and ticking, blues and whites; on a nice warm day or a cool one, add lashings of plaid and tweed to the chairs.

ABOVE Floral fabrics are ideal for outdoor cushions.
RIGHT Cane chairs and sofas have loose-fitted cushions and backs made of old cotton checks, stripes, and florals. Because it is roofed, this clapboarded patio forms an outdoor room.

LEFT It's not only the bottle of wine that makes this outdoor picnic in an olive grove inviting. The string and striped hammock and oversized cushion are both in bright colors, competing with the Mediterranean light.
BELOW Cheaper, plain tablecloths can be tweaked to suit a decorating scheme by sewing on ribbons. Here, the choice is a plain cotton one and a fancier omber style with picot edging. Note how the ribbons reappear on the vase of flowers.
OPPOSITE PAGE A slung wooden hammock gives character to the veranda of an East Hampton guest house. Its cotton cushions, in old striped and floral fabrics, match the dark green paint of the woodwork.

Small outdoor spaces in the center of cities offer the opportunity for a touch of *rus in urbe*. If you have only a basement, give it a single bamboo, a tiny dribbling fountain, and a concrete shelf to use as a seat, with one thick white cushion on the seat and another at the back. Keep all the colors cool, for it is in the center of the city where you need most calm. Alternatively, imitate the quiet courtyards of Moorish Spain or Florentine palazzi by adding comfortable piles of cushions to built-in seats or iron chairs grouped around an ornamental fountain and hanging baskets of green ferns and exotic leaves.

Even in midwinter, when a well-heated garden room beckons on a rare sunny day, the atmosphere should be summery. Keep the color scheme simple, ideally reflecting the planting of the garden beyond. Green and white are obvious choices; you could add gentian blue and citrus yellow to give the impression of ultramarine and white bluebells and Welsh poppies growing among the ivies outside; or stick to a couple of shades of bright red to startle among the green—but never be tempted to go for a riot of color in fabrics. The result will be as messy as a riot of color in a flowerbed.

For shade in the real outdoors, choose plants carefully grown over netting or big white canvas umbrellas (and you could buy an overhead mobile gas heater to take advantage of sunny spring and fall days). Any blinds used to shade the glass roof in a solarium or garden room should be practical and unobtrusive—wooden slats, pinoleum, or plain, natural canvas—because it is preferable to avoid drawing attention to the roof at the expense of the comfortable furnishings below.

FABRIC CARE

I've written in earlier parts of the book about choosing the right fabric for the job—and it is crucial. Unless you are devoted to shabby chic, all textiles should be meticulously clean. Modern fabrics make this simple: if they can't be laundered, they can be dry-cleaned, with the caveat that it is simpler to dry-clean large volumes of washable fabrics than to wash them. Otherwise, the washer may explode, the fabric come out only patchily clean, and the ironing fail to remove all the wrinkles.

When you buy any new fabric, ask how it can be cleaned. Make sure that any accessories you add—tassels, braiding, borders—will react in the same way. You don't want to have to unpick bits before the whole is cleaned. Ask, too, about whether cottons for slipcovers, curtains, and dust ruffles are likely to shrink—even if the answer is no, have them laundered before they are made. Find out about colorfastness and reaction to strong sunlight. For tailored upholstery, find specialized dry-cleaners to work in your home.

Some antique fabrics are as easy to care for as modern fabrics: old linen towels, sheets, and monochrome hangings can cope with a session in the washing machine. Other textiles, such as paisley shawls, antique toiles,

and heavy wool curtains, can be carefully dry-cleaned. Materials such as wool embroideries, lace, and heavy silks can be washed by hand at a cool temperature in pure soapflakes. I know that some antiques dealers put their patchwork quilts into washing machines on a cool cycle but I have never dared to do so myself. If you are buying such an item from a dealer, ask at the time about how to care for it—but take any advice with a pinch of salt, on the grounds that the dealer is trying to make a sale. Most cottons can be washed in a machine, but the colors should be checked in advance for fastness. Do a dummy run, if you can. It's preferable to treat a quilt as an ornament and take it off before going to bed.

There are trained conservators who will repair any antique fabric for you—at enormous cost and delays. If you want to make a repair yourself, always use the same fiber for the sewing thread as in the fabric: silk with silk, wool with wool, cotton with cotton.

Keep woolens in storage with mothballs near, but not touching, them. Fine textiles should be wrapped in acid-free tissue paper and given some ventilation to keep them free from mold. Inspect them regularly and change how they are folded. It may seem like a lot of effort, but it's worth it.

RIGHT A small gingham checked cotton has been used for this quickly made kitchen shade. its position means that the fabric should be easy to remove and wash.
FAR RIGHT A large gingham check is perfectly at ease in this formal living room. Added clout has been given by the bobble trim and fabric ties to poles, which must be as easily cleaned as the curtains.
OPPOSITE PAGE If you can find two fabrics that are a close—but not exact—match, use them for upholstery and curtaining. But pale shades are a bad idea if upholstery is in daily use.

PRACTICALITIES

equipment and techniques
The projects on the following pages—which range from simple curtains to a fitted chair cover—vary in the level of experience required, but most of the techniques involved in making them will be familiar from dressmaking. The equipment needed is minimal, but to help you to achieve lasting and professional results, it is worth investing in the best possible tools and materials.

BASIC SEWING KIT

Sewing machine
Modern electronic sewing machines have many advanced stitching features—but most soft furnishings require only a basic straight stitch and a zigzag for neatening seams. Always use a sharp needle and match its thickness to the weight of the fabric. The finest needles have the lowest numbers—so use size 8 for sheer curtains, 12 for most projects, and size 16 for heavy canvas.

Scissors
A selection of scissors is essential for anyone who is serious about making cushions, curtains, and other furnishings. Each pair should be kept for its own purpose:
Dressmaking shears with long blades are used for cutting fabric and should be kept well sharpened. The handles are bent at an angle so they can cut accurately.
Sewing scissors are smaller and have straight handles. Use these for trimming seams and clipping corners.
Embroidery scissors have short, sharp-pointed blades, which makes them ideal for trimming thread and notching seam allowances.
Paper scissors should be kept specially for cutting out patterns and templates.

Iron
Hems and seams must be pressed well, so you need a good steam iron and a large ironing board. Use a cleaning cloth to remove any build-up and clean the iron regularly. A dressmaker's sleeve board is useful for detailed work.

Needles
Hand-sewing needles come in various sizes for different tasks. Medium-length sharps are best for general sewing and basting, and shorter betweens can be used for slipstitch. Crewel needles have an extra-long eye designed for embroidery threads.

Thimble
A flat-top metal thimble should be used to protect the fingers when basting heavy fabrics together, but it may take a while to get used to.

Dressmaker's pins
These can be used for fine fabrics; larger glass-headed pins show up better on thicker material. Check that they are made from rustless steel.

Sewing thread
Always choose thread made from the same weight and fiber as the fabric being stitched. Mercerized cotton has a smooth surface and should be used for stitching cotton and linen.

Polyester thread is finer and can be used for blends. Match the color as closely as possible, and choose a darker shade if an exact match is not possible.

Basting thread
A loosely spun thread can be used for basting. It is not mercerized, so it breaks easily and can be unpicked without damaging a finished seam. Use a contrasting color that shows up when the basting is being removed.

Marking tools
Tailor's chalk, which comes in a thin, solid block, produces a fine line that brushes away easily. Use white for dark fabrics and the colored versions to mark paler cloth.
Chalk pencils can be sharpened to a fine point for detailed marking.
Dressmaker's pens have water-soluble or light-sensitive ink that washes out or fades completely a few hours after use without leaving any marks.

Measurements
Precise measurement is vital, so obtain a good tape measure that will not stretch with use and become inaccurate. Conversions are not exact. **Always follow either the standard or the metric measurements** when making a project.

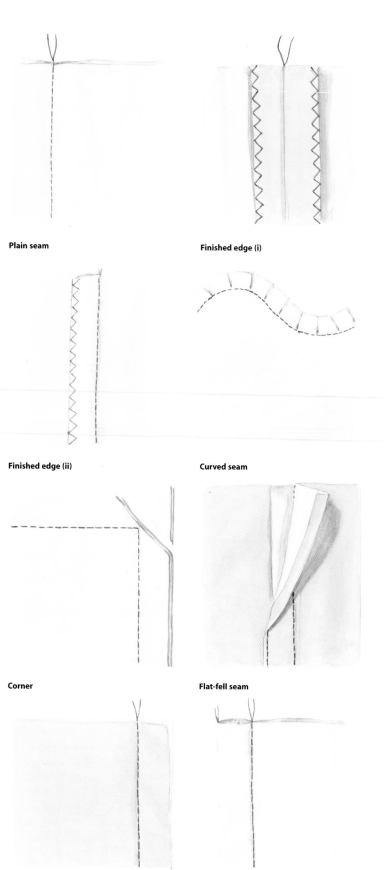

Plain seam

Finished edge (i)

Finished edge (ii)

Curved seam

Corner

Flat-fell seam

French seam (step 1)

French seam (step 2)

SEAMS

The extra fabric needed to join two pieces of fabric is given as the seam allowance. To keep it consistent, match the raw edges to the corresponding line on the bed of the sewing machine when stitching.

Plain seam Line up the two raw edges with right sides together. Pin at 2–4in (5–10cm) intervals, inserting the pins at right angles to the fabric or parallel to the edge. Baste, then machine stitch along the seam line. Press the seam open or to one side as directed and take out the basting.

Finished edge The cut edge of a plain seam may fray, especially if an item is washed. To prevent this, a line of zigzag or overlock stitch can be worked along each raw edge before seaming if the seam is to be pressed open (i). If the seam is to be pressed to one side, the seam allowance can be trimmed and the two edges joined together with a zigzag (ii).

Curved seam The allowance on a curved seam has to be trimmed back to $\frac{1}{3}$ in (1cm) and clipped so that the seam will lie flat. For an outside curve, make small notches; on an inside curve, clip a short distance into the seam allowance at regular intervals.

Corner To sew around a right-angled corner, stitch to the end of the seam allowance. Lift the presser foot, leaving the needle down. Turn the fabric 90 degrees, and continue stitching. Clip off the corner to within $\frac{1}{16}$ in (2mm) of the stitching before turning right side out so it will lie flat.

Flat-fell seam This seam shows on the right side as two parallel rows of stitches. With wrong sides facing, make a plain seam as above, then trim one seam allowance to $\frac{1}{4}$ in (6mm). Press under $\frac{1}{8}$ in (3mm) along the other allowance and baste the fold to the main fabric over the shortened edge. Machine stitch close to fold.

French seam Used for joining lightweight or sheer fabrics, this seam encloses the raw edges on the wrong side. With wrong sides together, seam the fabric $\frac{3}{8}$ in (8mm) from the edge. Trim the allowance to $\frac{1}{4}$ in (6mm) and fold the right sides together. Stitch again, $\frac{3}{8}$ in (8mm) from the edge.

HEMS

The finish to the lower edge of a piece of fabric depends on its weight:

Single hem Used for heavier linens and upholstery fabrics. Zigzag the raw edge and press the turning up to the required length on the wrong side. Pin and baste, then sew in place by hand or machine just below the zigzag.

Double hem Consists of one narrow and one deeper turning or two equal turnings, which give a firmer edge to finer fabrics. Press under ¼ in (6mm) along the raw edge, then turn up to length as directed. Pin and baste, then either machine stitch close to the inner fold or finish by hand. A machine stitch is used for chair covers, but curtain hems are hand finished for a better result.

MITERS

When two hems meet at right angles, the surplus fabric should be finished with a mitre to avoid a bulky corner.

Single hem Press under the turnings along each edge, then unfold them. Fold the corner inward at a right angle so the creases line up to make a square. Refold the hems, then slipstitch the folded edges together.

Double hem For two double hems of equal depth, press under both turnings. Unfold the second fold only, then turn in the corner, refold, and stitch as above. If one hem is deeper than the other, follow the method for an angled miter described on pages 158–59.

HAND STITCHING

All the projects in this section are stitched by machine, but hand sewing is vital for basting and finishing hems, miters, and some seams.

Slipstitch Used to join two folded edges or to secure a folded hem. Bring the needle out through the fold and pick up two threads of the other fabric. Pass the needle back through the fold for ¼ in (6mm) and repeat to the end.

Herringbone stitch Creates a flat, unobtrusive hem for curtains. Bring the needle up inside the hem and make a diagonal stitch up to the right, then a short horizontal stitch to the left. Work a diagonal stitch down to the right and, taking the needle through the top layer of the hem, make a short horizontal stitch to the left. Repeat these two stitches to continue.

Stab stitch A firm stitch used to secure two or more layers of fabric. Bring the needle up through all the layers, then take it back down ¹⁄₁₆ in (2mm) away.

Buttonhole stitch Mark a line the length of your button and outline it with running stitch. Cut along the line and anchor the thread on the wrong side. Insert the needle at the top left corner and bring it out through the opening. Loop the thread under the point and pull through. Repeat to the end and along the lower edge.

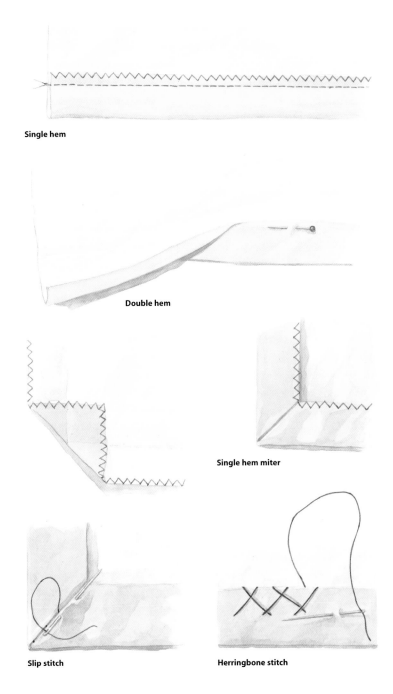

Single hem

Double hem

Single hem miter

Slip stitch

Herringbone stitch

Stab stitch

Buttonhole stitch

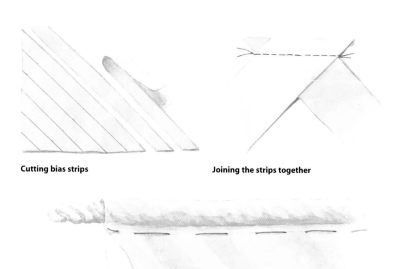

Cutting bias strips

Joining the strips together

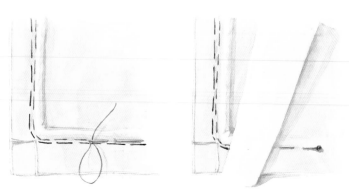

Covering the cord

Piping round a corner

Pinning second piece of fabric

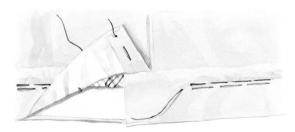

Piping on a curve

Joining a length of piping

PIPING AND CORDING

Piping is a folded length of fabric trim sewn into an edge, while cording is a soft cotton cord covered with a narrow strip of fabric. Both are sewn into a seam to make the seam more hard-wearing and to add a decorative line to a pillow cover or a slipcover that emphasizes the shape of the item. If it is not labeled "pre-shrunk," the cord should be washed at a high temperature before it is used. Piping cord is available in several thicknesses: the most commonly used is size 4, which requires a 1½ in (4cm) wide strip of fabric.

Covering the cord

Make a bias strip the same length as the cord. Mark a diagonal line on the fabric at 45 degrees to the edge. Draw a series of lines parallel to this, 1½ in (4cm) apart, and cut along them. With right sides together, join the strips at right angles ½ in (1cm) from the edge. Press the seams open. With the right side out, fold the strip around the cord and pin, then baste in place ⅛ in (3mm) from the cord.

Piping or cording a seam

Pin, then baste the piping or cording to the right side of the fabric, lining up the raw edges. Cut ¼ in (6mm) notches into the seam allowance on both the bias strip and the main fabric to give a smooth line on a curved seam— or clip into the seam allowance on the bias strip at a corner. With right sides together, pin the second piece of fabric in place. Baste, then machine stitch, using a zipper foot to sew close to the cord. Unpick the basting.

Making a join in a round of cording

A join in a continuous length of cording, or in a round of cording, can be made inconspicuous by positioning it next to a seam line.

Baste the cording in place, leaving a 1 in (2.5cm) overlap on each side of the join. Remove the basting for 1¼ in (3cm) at each loose end. Trim the cord so the ends butt and stitch them together loosely. Baste under the end of one bias strip so it lines up with the seam. Fold it over the other strip and baste both ends in place. Machine stitch as close to the cord as possible, using a zipper foot.

ZIPPERS

Zippers are available with either metal or plastic teeth, and come in a range of lengths and colors. To insert a zipper in a flat seam, pin and baste the two sides together along the seam allowance, then machine stitch each end, leaving a central gap ½ in (1.5cm) longer than the zipper. Reinforce both ends of the stitching. Press the seam open. Close the zipper, then baste it in place on the wrong side of the opening. Stitch the zipper in place from the right side, using the zipper foot to sew ⅛ in (3mm) from the teeth.

MACHINE APPLIQUÉ

Appliquéd motifs on home furnishings may need to be dry-cleaned or laundered, so they should be hard-wearing. A lasting finish can be created by joining them to the background fabric with iron-on bonding web and finishing the raw edges with machine stitch.

Draw the motif to full size, reversing the outline if it is not symmetrical, and trace it through onto the paper side of the bonding web. Cut the shape out roughly and place it, adhesive side down, onto the wrong side of the appliqué fabric. Iron in place following the manufacturer's instructions. Cut out carefully around the pencil outline, then peel away the backing paper. Position the motif on the background fabric, adhesive side down, and iron in place as directed.

Thread the machine to match the appliqué and adjust to a medium-width satin stitch. Working steadily, sew around the motif so the stitches cover the raw edge completely. Decrease the width of the stitch as you approach a corner or point to create a neat, tapered finish.

Iron-on stencil

Machine satin stitch

MEASURING A WINDOW FOR CURTAINS

Before you start to measure a window, the curtain hardware—rod, pole, or track—should be in place.

Width (A) Measure from the center of the window to the end of the pole. If the fixture is made in two parts, add extra for the overlap. Some fixtures have an angled return at each corner to accommodate the fabric when the curtains are open; add this length if necessary.

Length (B) Measure from the top edge of the track or the loops on the rings to the floor—or, for a shorter curtain, measure to just below the sill.

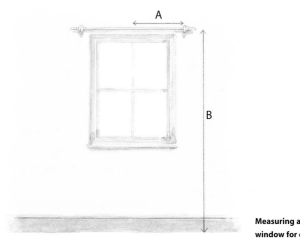

Measuring a window for curtains

PATTERNED CURTAIN FABRICS

Matching repeats

Patterned fabrics need to be matched across both curtains to make a pair and also when two lengths are joined to make a wide curtain. Measure the depth of the pattern repeat and add this to each length when calculating the fabric required. When cutting out the fabric, make sure each piece starts at the same point on the design.

Joining fabric widths

Patterned fabrics should be joined so the design matches horizontally across the seam. Press under the seam allowance on one side and pin the fold to the second length so the patterns line up. Baste together with a long slipstitch. Fold right sides together and machine stitch along the basted line. Finish the raw edges. A center seam can look clumsy. It can be avoided by cutting the second length of fabric into two panels and sewing one panel to each side of the first length.

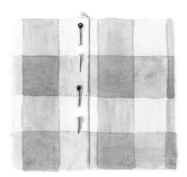

Joining patterned fabric

Joining fabric widths

unlined curtains

Unlined café-style curtains are usually made from a lighter-weight fabric than lined curtains, which allows daylight to filter through. Ready-made tapes designed to create instant pleated headings are easy to use—but it is worth making headings by hand, in the traditional way, because they give a crisper, more professional finish and can be adapted to create accurate pleats on striped or checked fabrics. Buckram—coarse cloth stiffened with size—gives rigidity to the headings.

Materials and equipment

lightweight to midweight fabric

matching sewing thread

dressmaker's pins

heading buckram 4in (10cm) deep

basic sewing kit

tailor's chalk

curtain hooks

Measuring and cutting out

The finished size of each curtain depends on the shape of the window and the type of curtain rod or pole used. (For advice on measuring a window, see page 157.) The final width = A; the final length = B.

Calculating the pleat allowance

The pleats are 5in (12cm) apart, and there should be as many pleats as gaps between them, including one half-gap at each end. To find out the number of pleats, divide A by 5in (12cm) and round up or down to the nearest whole number. Multiply this figure by 6in (15cm) to find out how much extra fabric is needed to make the pleats.

Curtain panel

If necessary, join one or more fabric widths to make the panel the correct size. (For advice on joining fabric widths, see page 157.)

width = A *plus* pleat allowance *plus* 4in (12cm) hem allowance *plus* overlap and allowances if required
depth = B *plus* 4$\frac{1}{2}$in (11cm) heading allowance *plus* 6in (16cm) hem allowance

Buckram

length = 1in (2cm) shorter than width of curtain panel

Calculating the total length of fabric required

Divide the width of the curtain panel by the width of the chosen fabric and round up to the nearest whole number. Multiply by the depth of the curtain panel, then by the number of curtains required. Allow an extra 1in (3cm) for each yard of non-preshrunk fabric. Remember to add any extra fabric needed to match the repeats on a patterned fabric (see page 157).

1 For each curtain, turn under and press a 1in (3cm) double hem along each side edge and a 3in (8cm) double hem along the bottom edge.

2 Mark three points with pins: the corner, the inside edge of the side turning where it meets the hem, and the corresponding point on the hem.

3 Unfold all the creases, then refold one turning along each edge. Fold the corner in so all three pins line up.

4 Press lightly, then refold and pin down the second turnings. Slipstitch the two sides of the miter together, from the corner inward.

5 Pin and baste the side and bottom hems. Machine or slipstitch the side hems, and slipstitch or herringbone stitch the bottom hem.

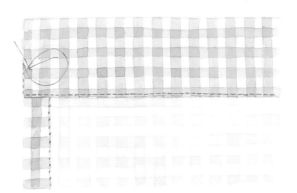

6 Press under a ½ in (1cm) turning along the top raw edge. Starting ½ in (1cm) in from one corner, pin the top edge of the buckram under the fold. Baste and machine stitch it in place. Fold the buckram to the wrong side and press along the fold.

7 Slipstitch together the side edges of the fold.

8 Using tailor's chalk, mark the positions of the pleats and the gaps between them along the wrong side of the top edge.

9 Pin two pleat lines together to make a large pleat. Baste and machine stitch on the right side to just below the bottom edge of the buckram.

10 Hand pleat the fabric into three equal-sized small folds, then press them into position. Pin, baste, and machine stitch across the folds ½ in (1cm) below the bottom edge of the buckram, at right angles to the pleat lines.

11 Sew a curtain hook securely to the top of each pleat, on the wrong side of the heading. If the curtain is to hang from decorative rings on a pole, the top of the hooks should be ½ in (1cm) below the top edge of the curtain. If the curtain is to hang from a track, the top of the hooks should be positioned 2in (5cm) down, so the track is concealed when the curtains are closed.

door curtains

A minimal amount of sewing is needed to create these curtains. Each panel is a simple rectangle, hemmed along each side and gathered at the top and bottom. The gingham curtains are drawn up with elastic and pinned in place, while the more formal folds of the plain curtains are created by using sprung curtain wire. Washable lightweight and sheer cotton upholstery or dressmaking fabrics are most suitable because they hang in fine folds. Small prints, solid colors, or geometric stripes and checks work best; large-scale patterns get lost when gathered.

Materials and equipment

basic sewing kit

cotton fabric

matching sewing thread

for the gingham curtains

narrow braid elastic

small safety pin

thumbtacks

for the plain curtains

sprung curtain wire

heavy wire cutters

four screw-eyes and
four cup hooks for each curtain

awl

Measuring and cutting out

The finished curtain should overlap the glass or mesh by 1in (3cm) at each side.

width = 1½ to 2 times the width of door panel (depending on weight of fabric) *plus* 2½in (6cm) overlap *plus* 1½in (4cm) hem allowance

length = depth of panel *plus* 2in (6cm) overlap *plus* 1½in (4cm) clearance *plus* 2½in (6cm) for the cased headings

Making the curtains

1 Iron the fabric to remove any creases. Press under ½in (1cm) along each long edge. Press under another ½in (1cm) to make a double hem, then pin, baste, and machine stitch close to the inner fold. If the fabric is not the same on both sides, make the hems on the right side of the curtain.

2 Press under ½in (1cm) along the bottom edge, then press under another ¾in (2cm). Pin, baste, and machine stitch close to the inner fold to form a narrow channel or cased heading. Do the same at the top edge and remove any loose threads.

Hanging the gingham curtains

1 Cut a length of elastic braid 1½in (4cm) shorter than the width of the door panel. Put a safety pin on one end and pass it along the bottom casing. Pull the elastic through until the loose end is in line with the opening, then stab stitch it securely in place through the front and back of the casing.

2 Bring the pin out at the other end and sew the end of the elastic to the casing. Thread the top casing in the same way.

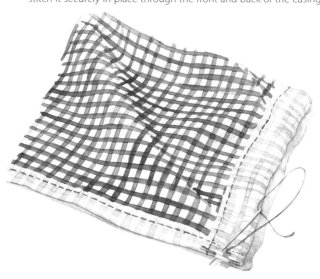

3 With hems and casings facing the door, attach the curtain to the inside of the cabinet using three thumbtacks at top edge and three at the bottom.

Hanging the plain curtains

1 Mark four points on the back of the cupboard door, 3cm (1in) from each corner of the opening. Use a bradawl to make a hole at each mark and screw the hooks into the door so that they face upwards.

2 Twist a screw-eye into one end of the sprung wire and loop it over a hook. Stretch the wire across to the second hook—it should be taut but not too tight—and make a pencil mark on the wire where they meet.

3 Cut the wire to length and twist the second eye in place. Do the same with the second piece of wire.

4 Feed the two wires into the top and bottom casings; the fabric will gather up as it goes through.

5 Hook the top wire in place so the hems and casings face the door, then slip the bottom screw-eyes over the hooks.

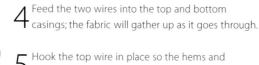

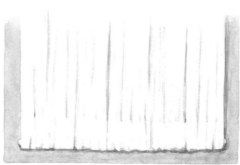

6 Ease the casing over the screw-eyes to conceal them and adjust the gathers so they lie regularly in parallel folds.

Roman shade

This type of Roman shade is made from a lined rectangular panel, weighted by a lath, with cords on the reverse side. It is hung on a strip of wood, which can be set in a window recess or mounted on a wall. A close-woven cotton fabric is easy to sew and will endure heavy use.

Materials and equipment

ticking or similar striped fabric

white lining fabric

½in (1.5cm) plastic rings

matching sewing thread

nylon shade cord

shade acorn

basic sewing kit

dressmaker's pins

long ruler

tailor's chalk

wooden lath, ¾in (2cm) shorter than finished width of shade

3 small screw-eyes

1¼ x 1¼in (3cm x 3cm) strip of wood, ¼in (5mm) shorter than finished width of shade

staple gun

small safety pin

two small angle brackets, screws, and anchors or four long screws and anchors

cleat and screws

drill

screwdriver

If the shade is to be mounted on the wall, the ends and underside of the batten will be visible, so the wood should be painted to match the color of the shade.

Measuring

If shade is to hang in a window recess
width (A) = width of recess *minus* ¾in (2cm)
length (B) = from top of recess to sill

If shade is to hang outside a window recess or over a frame
width (A) = width of frame or recess *plus* 2½in (6cm)
length (B) = from top of wood strip to 1in (3cm) below bottom edge of frame or sill

Cutting out

Shade and lining alike
width = A *plus* 1½in (4cm)
depth= B *plus* 5in (12cm)

Three cords cut to the following lengths
2B, 2B *plus* ¼ A, 2B *plus* A

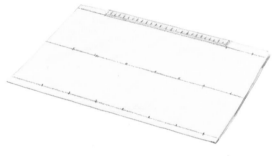

1 Mark a chalk line down the center of the right side of the lining, then draw two more lines 2in (5cm) in from each long edge. Starting 6in (15cm) up from the bottom edge, make a series of marks at 12in (30cm) intervals along each line. Leave a space of at least 8in (20cm) at the top edge to accommodate the shade when it is open.

2 Hand stitch a small plastic ring securely to each of the marks, then brush away the chalk lines.

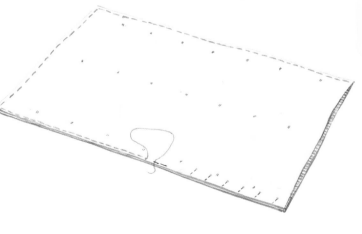

3 With right sides together, pin the long side edges and top edge of the shade and the lining. Baste, then machine stitch, leaving a seam allowance of ¾in (2cm). Clip the corners, turn right side out, and press.

4 Make a casing to hold the lath at the bottom of the shade on the same side as the tapes. Press under a ³⁄₄ in (2cm) turning along the raw edge, then press under a further 1¹⁄₄ in (4cm) turning. Baste, then machine stitch, ¹⁄₈ in (3mm) from the inside fold.

5 Slip the lath inside the casing and secure the open ends with slipstitch.

6 If the shade is to fit in a recess, drill four equally spaced holes through the batten from top to bottom. Mark the center back of the strip of wood. Then put the screw-eyes in the underside so one lies at the top of each line of rings.

7 Press a ³⁄₄ in (2cm) turning to the wrong side along the shade's top edge. With the right side of the shade facing down, staple the center top of the shade to the center back of the strip of wood, so the fold lies along the back edge of the batten. Continue stapling toward each end: the fabric will overlap the ends slightly.

8 With the shade laid flat and the rings uppermost, thread the cords in order from the shortest to the longest. Fasten a small safety pin to one end of the first cord. Thread the cord through the first screw-eye on the left, then down through the first line of rings. Undo the pin and sew the end of the cord securely to the final ring. (For a shade that pulls up from the left, start with the first screw-eye on the right.)

9 Thread the second cord through the first and center screw-eyes, then through the center line of rings. Attach the third cord in the same way, passing it through the preceding screw-eyes. Thread all the loose ends through the cord pull and adjust them so that they are the same length. Knot securely, trim, and slide the pull over the knot.

10 A wall-mounted shade is mounted on or above the window frame, using a small-angle bracket at each end of the strip. If the shade is to fit in a window recess, drill three holes into the top of the recess, in line with the holes in the strip of wood, and use long screws and anchors to mount it in place. Screw a cleat on or near the frame, on the same side as the cords.

linen bedspread

This lightweight summer bedcover is made from strips of linen that have been joined together with durable French seams and bound at the top and bottom edges with a contrasting dark fabric. The measurements given can be adapted to fit a bed of any width.

Materials and equipment

pale-colored linen

white linen

dark-colored linen

matching sewing thread

dressmaker's pins

sewing machine

sewing kit

Measuring

width (A) = width of bed *plus* 2 x height

length (B) = length of bed *plus* height

Cutting out

Panel of colored linen
(cut three)
width = 4C *plus* 1in (3cm)
seam allowance
length = B

Panel of white linen (cut two)
width = C *plus* 1in (3cm)
seam allowance
length = B

Binding (cut two)
width = 5in (12cm)
length = A *plus* 4in (10cm)

Panel widths Divide the finished width A by 14 to find width C, the width of the white panels. The colored panels are four times wider (4C) than the white panels.

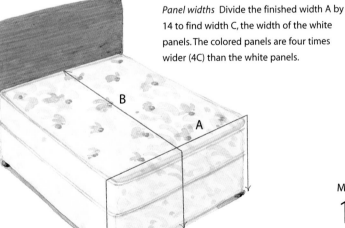

Making the bedspread

1 With wrong sides together, pin and baste one long edge of the first white panel to one long edge of the first colored panel.

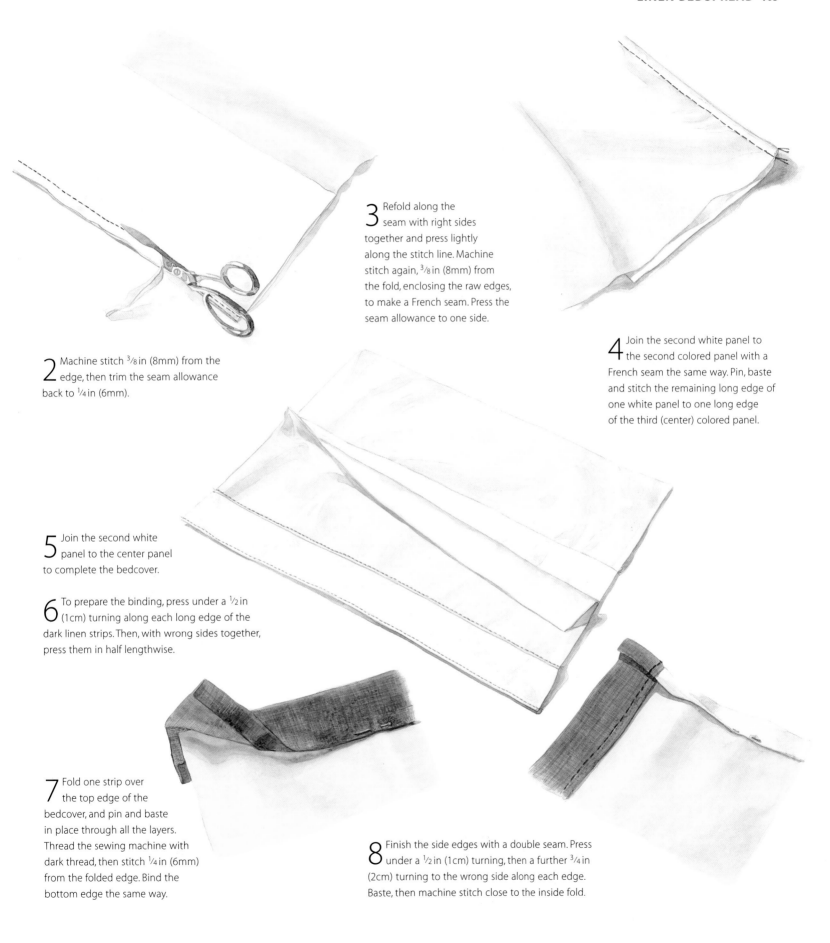

3 Refold along the
seam with right sides
together and press lightly
along the stitch line. Machine
stitch again, $^3/_8$ in (8mm) from
the fold, enclosing the raw edges,
to make a French seam. Press the
seam allowance to one side.

2 Machine stitch $^3/_8$ in (8mm) from the
edge, then trim the seam allowance
back to $^1/_4$ in (6mm).

4 Join the second white panel to
the second colored panel with a
French seam the same way. Pin, baste
and stitch the remaining long edge of
one white panel to one long edge
of the third (center) colored panel.

5 Join the second white
panel to the center panel
to complete the bedcover.

6 To prepare the binding, press under a $^1/_2$ in
(1cm) turning along each long edge of the
dark linen strips. Then, with wrong sides together,
press them in half lengthwise.

7 Fold one strip over
the top edge of the
bedcover, and pin and baste
in place through all the layers.
Thread the sewing machine with
dark thread, then stitch $^1/_4$ in (6mm)
from the folded edge. Bind the
bottom edge the same way.

8 Finish the side edges with a double seam. Press
under a $^1/_2$ in (1cm) turning, then a further $^3/_4$ in
(2cm) turning to the wrong side along each edge.
Baste, then machine stitch close to the inside fold.

chair back and tie-on seat cover

This informal Scandinavian-style chair back and seat cover, which match the fabrics used on the bed, have practical origins. Similar two-part covers were first used to protect expensively upholstered furniture from dust or bright sunlight, but they eventually became fashionable in their own right. All padded chairs vary in shape and are often contoured, so the seat template has to be modeled directly over the chair. Take time doing this to make sure you achieve a perfect fit.

Materials and equipment

60in (150cm) gingham upholstery fabric 60in (150cm) wide
56in (140cm) cotton tape for ties
basic sewing kit
matching sewing thread
pencil and dressmaker's graph paper
dressmaker's pins

Measuring up and cutting out

Chair back (cut two)

width = top edge measured from center of outside edges of struts (A) *plus* ³⁄₄ in (2cm) *plus* 1in (3cm) seam allowance

depth = from center of top of strut to ³⁄₄ in (2cm) from seat (B) *plus* 1¹⁄₂ in (4cm) seam and hem allowance

E = depth of cushioned part

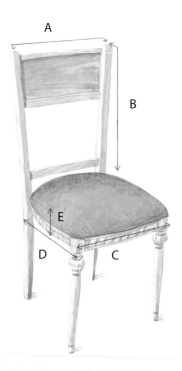

Cutting out the seat cover

1 Measure the width (C *plus* 2E) and depth (D *plus* 2E). Cut the paper to this size and pin it to the seat. Fold and pin a dart at each front corner.

2 Use a pencil to mark on the paper the inside points of the back struts. Cut diagonally from the back corners to these points, then cut out shapes to fit around the base of each strut.

3 Pin the side drops to the seat and trim so they line up with the back corners of the chair legs. Mark the bottom edge of the seat with a pencil line. Unpin the pattern.

4 Cut around the pencil outline and along the folds at the front corners. Fold the template in half widthwise to check that it is symmetrical. Pin it to the fabric, following the grain.

5 Cut out, adding a seam allowance of ¹⁄₂ in (1.5cm) at each corner and a 1in (3cm) hem along each drop.

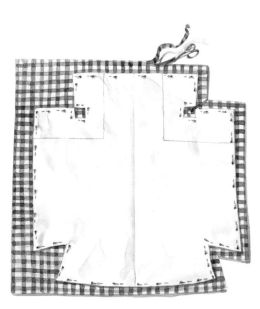

6 The back corners are reinforced with facings in the same fabric. To make the pattern, draw a line 3in (8cm) from one corner of the seat template and cut out. Cut two pieces, allowing an extra ¹⁄₂ in (1.5cm) all around.

Making the seat cover

1 Cut the tape into four 14in (35cm) lengths. Baste in place on the back and side drops ¾in (2cm) away from the corners.

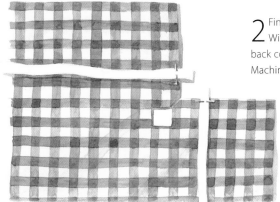

2 Finish the two long straight edges of each facing. With right sides together, pin the facings to the back corners of the seat cover, enclosing the tapes. Machine stitch ½in (1.5cm) from the inside edge.

3 Clip the seam allowance at the inside corners and trim the outside corners. Turn the facings right side out and topstitch the seam.

4 Finish the edges of the front and side drops. With right sides together, pin and baste, and machine stitch ½in (1.5cm) from the edge. Press the seams open and turn right side out.

5 Press under a ½in (1.5 cm) double hem around the outside edge, and pin and baste in place. Tie the cover in place, check that the hem is level, and machine stitch close to the inside fold. Press the cover.

Making the chair back

1 Finish the top and side edges of each rectangle. With right sides together, pin and baste the finished edges together, then machine stitch, making a seam allowance of ½in (1.5cm).

2 Slip the cover over the chair. Fold the top and side seams together at one top corner to form a triangle, then pin them together along the edge of the chair back. Stitch along this line, then trim the seam allowance to ⅜in (8mm) and finish. Dart the other corner in the same way and press the seams open.

3 Press a ½in (1.5cm) double hem around the lower edge, then baste and machine stitch in place. Turn right side out and press.

slipcover for a dining chair

This cover is constructed from a series of rectangles to give a close, tailored fit. The contrasting border and appliquéd motif add elegant finishing touches. Box pleats at each corner accommodate the splay of the legs, and no additional fastenings are required. This design is suitable for a simple upright chair with a narrow metal or wooden frame without any upholstery or carving. The back should be no deeper than 1¼in (3cm).

Materials and equipment

2¾yds (2.5m) plain upholstery fabric 60in (150cm) wide
20in (50cm) contrast fabric 60in (150cm) wide
3¼yds (3m) medium piping cord
basic sewing kit
pattern graph paper
dressmaker's pins
matching sewing thread
tailor's chalk

Measuring

Take each measurement from the widest point of the chair.

Inside back
top width = top edge from center of side struts (A)
bottom width = back edge from center of side struts (C)
depth = from center top of side strut to seat (B)

Seat
back width = back edge from center of side struts (C)
front width = front edge from corner to corner (D)
depth = side edge from front corner to center of back strut (E)

Outside back
top width = top edge from center of side struts (A)
center and bottom widths = back edge from center of side struts (C)
    plus 2 pleats (6in/16cm)
depth of back = from center top of side strut to seat (B)
depth of skirt = from top edge of seat to floor (F) *minus* border (4in/10cm)

Back border
width = as bottom width of outside back
depth = 5in (12cm)

Front skirt
width = front edge of seat from corner to corner (D)
    plus 2 pleats (6in/16cm)
depth = from top edge of seat to floor (F) *minus* border (4in/10cm)

Front border
width = as front skirt
depth = 5in (12cm)

Side skirt
width = side edge of seat from front corner to center of back strut (E)
    plus 6 pleats (18in/48cm)
depth = from top edge of seat to floor *minus* border (4in/10cm)

Side border
width = as side skirt
depth = 5in (12cm)

Cording
length = A + 2B + 2E + D (to fit around perimeter of the back and seat)
    plus 2in (5cm) to join the ends

For guidance on how to make the cording, see page 156.

Making the pattern and cutting out

1 Make a copy of the pattern diagram and fill in the measurements.

2 Draw the eight pieces full size on pattern paper and add a seam allowance of $\frac{1}{2}$in (1cm) around each shape.

3 Transfer the markings: the dotted lines indicate folds and the gray arrows show the direction of the fabric grain.

4 Mark a notch at the top of each fold line where shown by the small triangles on the diagram. Leave 3in (8cm) between one notch and the next (*a* to *f*).

5 Cut out the pieces and pin them around the chair to check their accuracy; make any necessary adjustments.

6 Lay the pattern pieces out on the fabric. Check that they all follow the grain of the fabric.

7 Cut out the fabric. Then clip a $\frac{1}{4}$in (6mm) notch at the top of each pleat where shown by the small triangles. Press and label each piece.

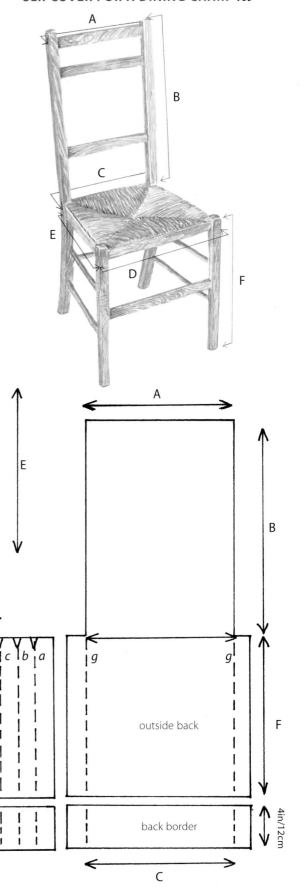

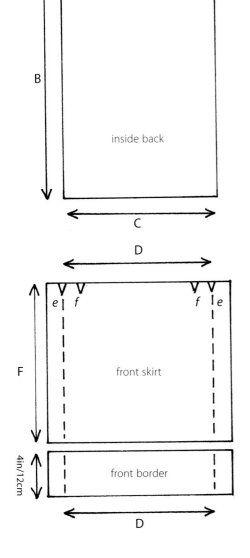

A

B

inside back

C

C

E

skirt

D

A

B

outside back

F

D

V V   V V
e f   f e

front skirt

F

4in/12cm front border

D

E

V V V V   V V V V
a b c d   d c b a

side skirt (cut two)

F

4in/12cm side border (cut two)

D

g   g

F

4in/12cm back border

C

Making the cover

The seam allowance throughout is ½ in (1.5cm).

1 Finish the top edge of the front border and the bottom edge of the front skirt. With right sides together, pin, baste, and machine stitch the two edges, then press the seam open.

2 Sew the borders onto the bottom of the two side skirts and the outside back panel the same way. Add any appliqué decoration to the outside back panel (see page 157).

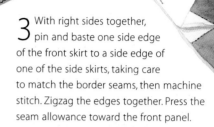

3 With right sides together, pin and baste one side edge of the front skirt to a side edge of one of the side skirts, taking care to match the border seams, then machine stitch. Zigzag the edges together. Press the seam allowance toward the front panel.

4 Join the other side edge of the front skirt to the other side skirt the same way.

5 Join the other side edges of the side skirts to the side edges of the outside back panel (lower half). Finish the seams and press toward the back panel. Turn cover right side out.

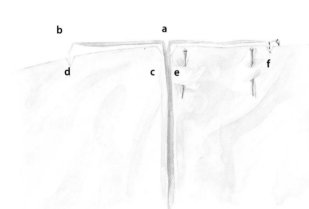

7 To make the back pleats, start at the top right corner of the side skirt. Fold along line **c** (see pattern diagram, page 169). Match notch **c** to notch **a** and notch **d** to notch **b**, then pin and stitch down the fold ½ in (1.5cm) from the edge. Turn the cover wrong side out.

8 Make the second half of the pleat by folding along the seam line and matching notch **a** to point **g**. Pin, baste, and machine stitch as far as the base of notch **a** ½ in (1.5cm) from the top edge. Make the other back pleat the same way.

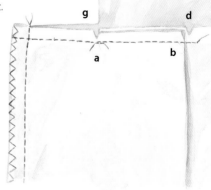

6 To make the front pleats, start at the top right corner of the front skirt. Fold along line **e**. Match notch **e** to notch **a**; line up notch **f** to the seam line and pin in place. Then match notch **c** to notch **a** and notch **d** to notch **b** and pin in place. Baste and machine stitch across the top of both folds ½ in (1.5cm) from the edge. Make the pleat at the top left corner the same way.

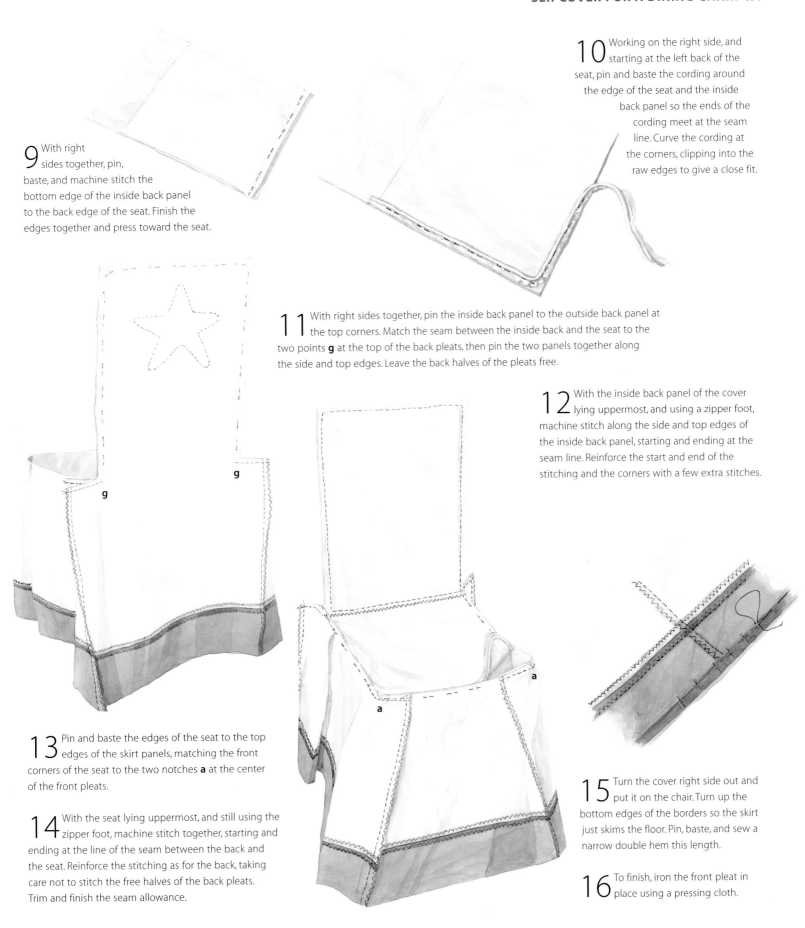

9 With right sides together, pin, baste, and machine stitch the bottom edge of the inside back panel to the back edge of the seat. Finish the edges together and press toward the seat.

10 Working on the right side, and starting at the left back of the seat, pin and baste the cording around the edge of the seat and the inside back panel so the ends of the cording meet at the seam line. Curve the cording at the corners, clipping into the raw edges to give a close fit.

11 With right sides together, pin the inside back panel to the outside back panel at the top corners. Match the seam between the inside back and the seat to the two points **g** at the top of the back pleats, then pin the two panels together along the side and top edges. Leave the back halves of the pleats free.

12 With the inside back panel of the cover lying uppermost, and using a zipper foot, machine stitch along the side and top edges of the inside back panel, starting and ending at the seam line. Reinforce the start and end of the stitching and the corners with a few extra stitches.

13 Pin and baste the edges of the seat to the top edges of the skirt panels, matching the front corners of the seat to the two notches **a** at the center of the front pleats.

14 With the seat lying uppermost, and still using the zipper foot, machine stitch together, starting and ending at the line of the seam between the back and the seat. Reinforce the stitching as for the back, taking care not to stitch the free halves of the back pleats. Trim and finish the seam allowance.

15 Turn the cover right side out and put it on the chair. Turn up the bottom edges of the borders so the skirt just skims the floor. Pin, baste, and sew a narrow double hem this length.

16 To finish, iron the front pleat in place using a pressing cloth.

tie-on pillow covers

Ties made from fabric, tape, or ribbon make a simple and decorative fastening for square or rectangular pillow covers. The open-ended cover looks especially effective with a contrasting color inside, while the pillowcase cover has a deep tuck-in flap on the inside that conceals the pillow form and holds it in place.

Open-ended cover
Materials and equipment

main fabric
plain pillow to go inside cover
basic sewing kit
matching sewing thread
dressmaker's pins
knitting needle

Measuring and cutting out

Front and back panels (cut two)
width = width of inner pillow (A)
plus 1in (3cm) seam allowance
depth = depth of inner pillow (B)
plus 1in (3cm) seam allowance

Facings (cut two)
width = 6in (15cm)
depth = B *plus* 1in (3cm)

Ties (cut four)
width = 3in (8cm)
length = 12in (30cm)

1 To make each of the four ties, fold the strip of fabric in half lengthwise, with right sides together. Machine stitch the long edge, leaving ½in (1.5cm) seam allowance, then sew across one short edge. Clip the end corners.

2 Turn each tie right side out. Ease the corners into shape using a knitting needle, and press.

3 Mark the positions of the ties on the front panel along the edge that will be the opening. Pin the ties to the right side, matching the raw edges, and baste in place. Do the same with the back panel.

4 Sew a narrow double hem along one long edge of each facing.

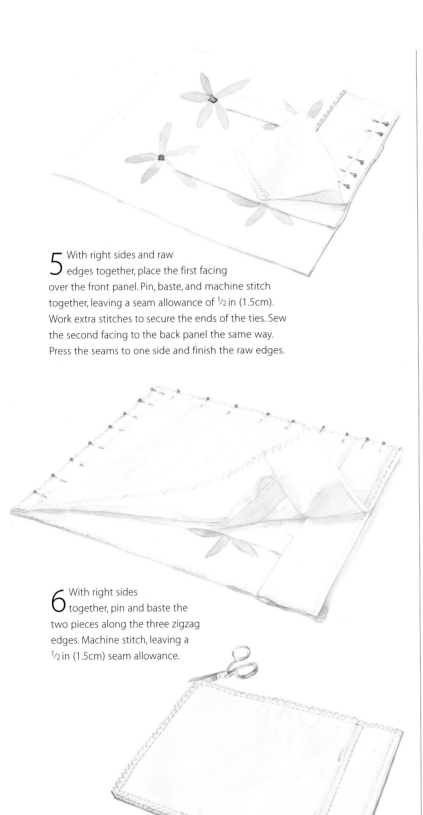

5 With right sides and raw edges together, place the first facing over the front panel. Pin, baste, and machine stitch together, leaving a seam allowance of ½ in (1.5cm). Work extra stitches to secure the ends of the ties. Sew the second facing to the back panel the same way. Press the seams to one side and finish the raw edges.

6 With right sides together, pin and baste the two pieces along the three zigzag edges. Machine stitch, leaving a ½ in (1.5cm) seam allowance.

7 Clip the end corners, then press the seams open. Turn the cover right side out and press the facings to the inside. Insert the contrasting pillow and tie the bows.

Pillowcase-ended cover

Materials and equipment

main fabric

pillow form

basic sewing kit

matching sewing thread

dressmaker's pins

Measuring and cutting out

Front and back (cut two)

width = width of pad (A)

plus 1in (3cm)

depth = depth of pad (B)

plus 1in (3cm)

Front facing

width = 5in (12cm)

depth = B *plus* 1in (3cm)

Back facing

width = 8in (20cm)

depth = B *plus* 1in (3cm)

Ties (cut four)

width = 4in (10cm)

length = 10in (25cm)

1 Attach ties and facings to front and back pieces as for open-ended cover up to step 5. Press the seams open and finish the raw edges.

2 With right sides together, pin and baste the remaining three edges of the front and back panels.

3 Fold the (longer) back facing across the back panel and baste it to the two side edges.

4 Fold the (shorter) front facing across the opening and over the ties, so it lies flat over the back facing. Pin and baste it in place, then machine stitch around all three edges, leaving a ½ in (1.5cm) seam allowance.

5 Clip the corners, then turn the cover right side out, and press. Insert the pillow form, tuck it under the back facing, and knot the ties.

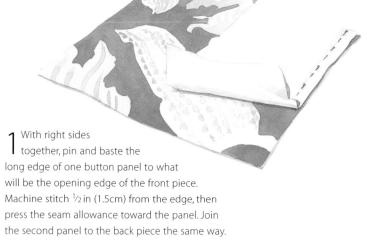

1 With right sides together, pin and baste the long edge of one button panel to what will be the opening edge of the front piece. Machine stitch ½ in (1.5cm) from the edge, then press the seam allowance toward the panel. Join the second panel to the back piece the same way.

buttoned pillow cover

A buttoned fastening can be made along one, two, three, or even four sides of a pillow cover. The buttons are sewn onto the back cover, and rows of buttonholes are worked on the front, parallel to the edges. The wide band of contrasting plain fabric at the opening has the effect of emphasizing the ornamental quality of the buttons.

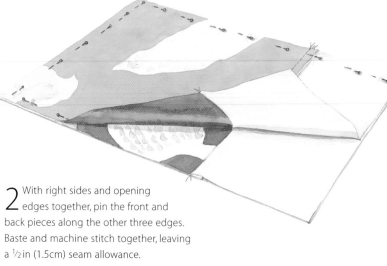

2 With right sides and opening edges together, pin the front and back pieces along the other three edges. Baste and machine stitch together, leaving a ½ in (1.5cm) seam allowance.

3 Clip the corners, then trim and finish the seam allowance.

Materials and equipment

main fabric
contrasting fabric
three buttons
rectangular pillow form
basic sewing kit
matching thread
dressmaker's pins

Measuring and cutting out

Front and back pieces (cut two of each)
width = ¾ width of pillow form (A)
plus 1in (3cm) seam allowance
depth = depth of pillow form (B)
plus 1in (3cm) seam allowance

Button panels (cut two)
width = ½ A *plus* 1in (3cm) seam allowance
depth = B *plus* 1in (3cm) seam allowance

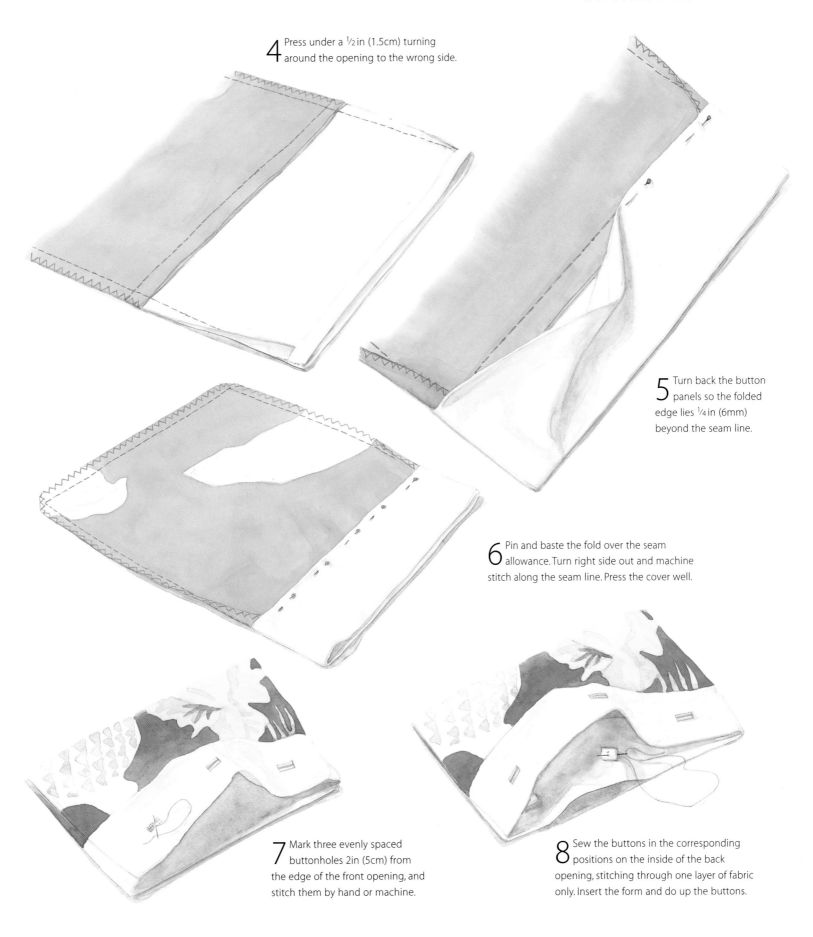

4 Press under a ½in (1.5cm) turning around the opening to the wrong side.

5 Turn back the button panels so the folded edge lies ¼in (6mm) beyond the seam line.

6 Pin and baste the fold over the seam allowance. Turn right side out and machine stitch along the seam line. Press the cover well.

7 Mark three evenly spaced buttonholes 2in (5cm) from the edge of the front opening, and stitch them by hand or machine.

8 Sew the buttons in the corresponding positions on the inside of the back opening, stitching through one layer of fabric only. Insert the form and do up the buttons.

bed bolster

This bed bolster is fastened with a long zipper: upholstery suppliers and notions counters sell zippers that can be cut to a specified length. To achieve a firm, well-stuffed appearance, the cover is cut the same size as the filling form, without any extra seam allowance.

Materials and equipment

a 48in (120cm) length of cotton ticking or striped furnishing fabric 60in (150cm) wide

72in (180cm) medium piping cord

matching zipper 12in (30cm) shorter than the length of the bolster

feather-filled bolster pad

basic sewing kit

matching sewing thread

dressmaker's pins

Measuring and cutting out

Main piece
width = length of bolster (A)
depth = circumference of end (B)

Circular end pieces (cut two)
diameter = diameter of bolster end (C)

Piping (make two lengths)
length = C *plus* 2in (5cm)

For guidance on how to make the piping, see page 156.

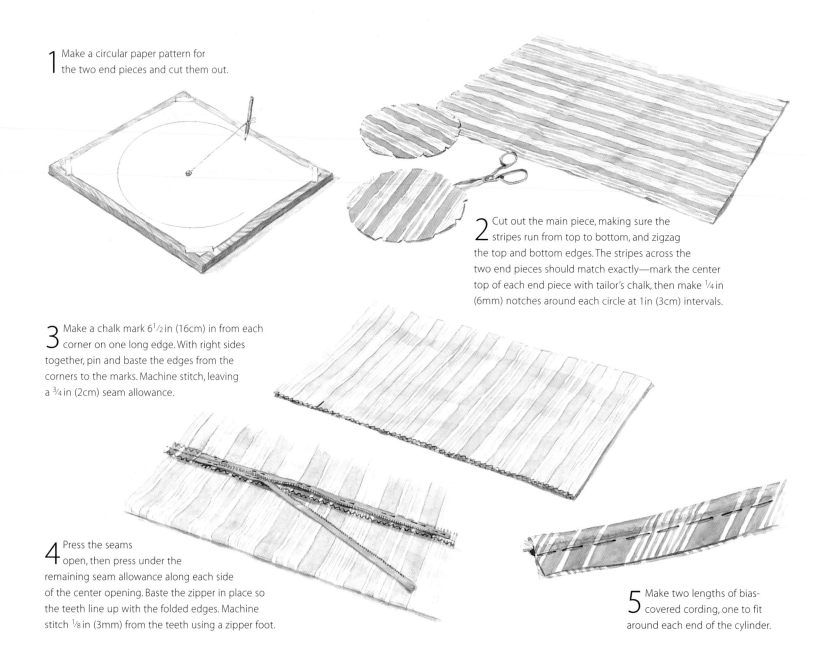

1 Make a circular paper pattern for the two end pieces and cut them out.

2 Cut out the main piece, making sure the stripes run from top to bottom, and zigzag the top and bottom edges. The stripes across the two end pieces should match exactly—mark the center top of each end piece with tailor's chalk, then make ¼in (6mm) notches around each circle at 1in (3cm) intervals.

3 Make a chalk mark 6½in (16cm) in from each corner on one long edge. With right sides together, pin and baste the edges from the corners to the marks. Machine stitch, leaving a ¾in (2cm) seam allowance.

4 Press the seams open, then press under the remaining seam allowance along each side of the center opening. Baste the zipper in place so the teeth line up with the folded edges. Machine stitch ⅛in (3mm) from the teeth using a zipper foot.

5 Make two lengths of bias-covered cording, one to fit around each end of the cylinder.

6 Pin the cording circles to the right side of the cover, lining up each join with the seam line.

7 Finish the joins (see page 156), then baste the cording in place. Machine stitch using a zipper foot.

8 Cut a series of notches about 1in (3cm) apart into the seam allowances of both the fabric and the cording at each end of the cover. Undo the zipper and turn the cover wrong side out.

9 With right sides together, pin the circular end pieces to the open ends of the cover, matching the center top of each to the seam line. Baste, then machine stitch close to the cord using a zipper foot.

10 Trim and finish the seam allowances. Turn right side out and press. Insert the bolster form and close the zipper.

drawstring bag

This colorful drawstring bag is made from a wide rectangle of fabric. The measurements can be scaled up or down to make bags of various sizes, which might be used to contain anything from the week's laundry to a pair of shoes.

Materials and equipment

40 x 30in (105 x 80cm) firm cotton fabric

1yd (1m) thick piping cord

12in (30cm) striped
grosgrain ribbon 2in (5cm) wide

basic sewing kit

tailor's chalk

dressmaker's pins

matching thread

tape

safety pin

1 Fold the fabric in half widthwise to find the center point of what will be the top edge. Using tailor's chalk, mark a short line at right angles to this point on the right side of the fabric.

2 With right sides together, fold the fabric again, then pin and baste the side and bottom edges together. Machine stitch, leaving a seam allowance of $^1/_2$ in (1.5cm), then finish the edges. Press the side seam to one side.

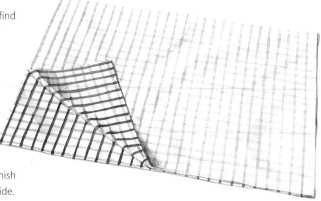

3 Press under $^1/_2$ in (1.5cm) along the top edge, then press under a further $1^1/_2$ in (4cm). This will form the drawstring casing.

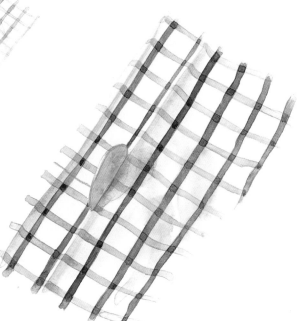

4 Turn the bag right side out and unfold the turnings. To make the opening for the drawstring, mark a $1^1/_4$ in (3cm) chalk line along the inner fold, across the first chalk line. Work a buttonhole by machine or hand (see page 155) along this line.

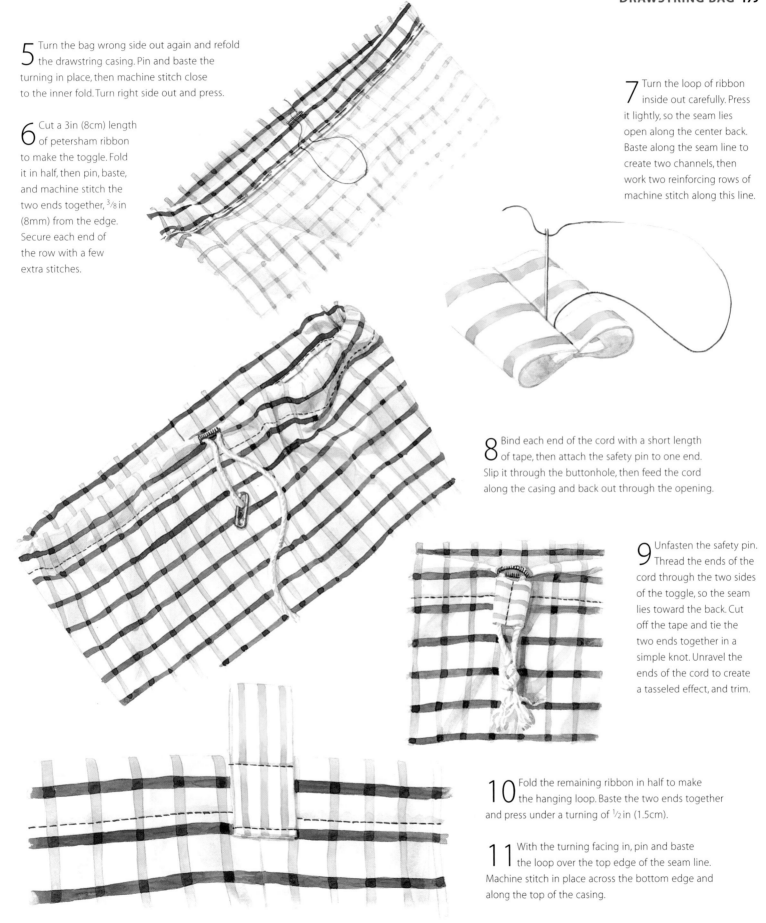

5 Turn the bag wrong side out again and refold the drawstring casing. Pin and baste the turning in place, then machine stitch close to the inner fold. Turn right side out and press.

6 Cut a 3in (8cm) length of petersham ribbon to make the toggle. Fold it in half, then pin, baste, and machine stitch the two ends together, $^3/_8$ in (8mm) from the edge. Secure each end of the row with a few extra stitches.

7 Turn the loop of ribbon inside out carefully. Press it lightly, so the seam lies open along the center back. Baste along the seam line to create two channels, then work two reinforcing rows of machine stitch along this line.

8 Bind each end of the cord with a short length of tape, then attach the safety pin to one end. Slip it through the buttonhole, then feed the cord along the casing and back out through the opening.

9 Unfasten the safety pin. Thread the ends of the cord through the two sides of the toggle, so the seam lies toward the back. Cut off the tape and tie the two ends together in a simple knot. Unravel the ends of the cord to create a tasseled effect, and trim.

10 Fold the remaining ribbon in half to make the hanging loop. Baste the two ends together and press under a turning of $^1/_2$ in (1.5cm).

11 With the turning facing in, pin and baste the loop over the top edge of the seam line. Machine stitch in place across the bottom edge and along the top of the casing.

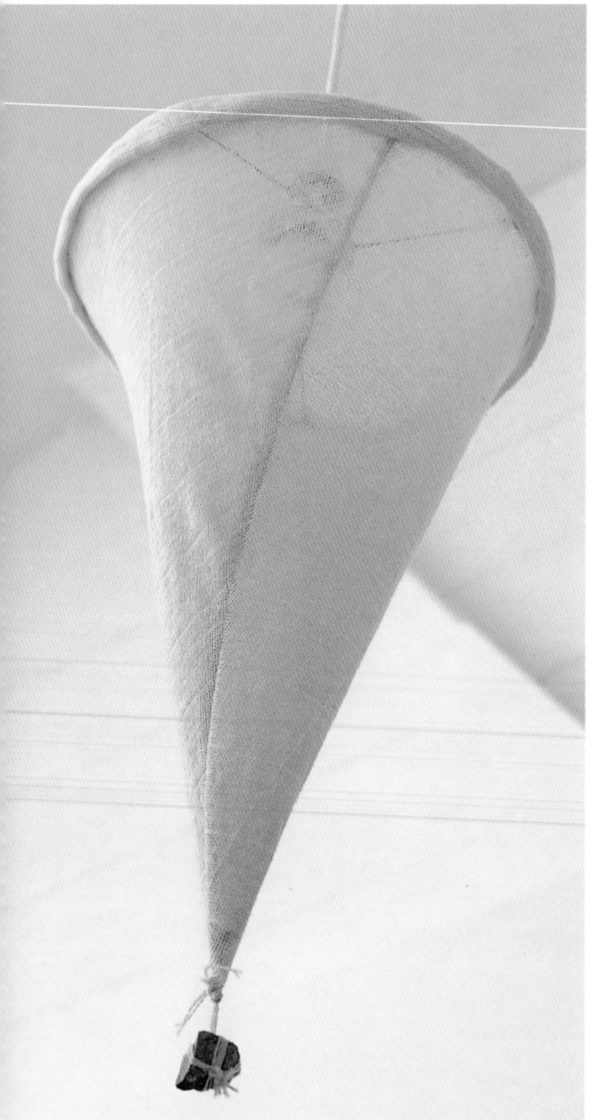

conical lampshade

This ceiling-mounted lampshade is stitched from a quarter-circle of fabric. Choose openweave linen or cotton to create a soft, diffused effect when it is lit, and remember to use a low-watt bulb. The pebble adds a final decorative touch to the point of the cone and also helps the shade hang properly.

Designed by Sheila Scholes

materials and equipment

10in (25cm) diameter metal ring
to fit over light fixture

22in (55cm) square of open-weave fabric

matching thread

tape measure

pencil

drawing board

masking tape

length of string and thumbtack

sheet of paper

matching bias binding

dressmaker's pins

small pebble

clear impact adhesive

tailor's chalk

ruler

1 Start by making a semicircular template. Cut a 22in (55cm) square of paper and tape it onto a drawing board. Tie one end of the string around the pencil, near to the point, and pin the other end to one corner of the paper, so the string is 22in (55cm) long. Holding the pencil upright, carefully draw an arc linking the two nearest corners.

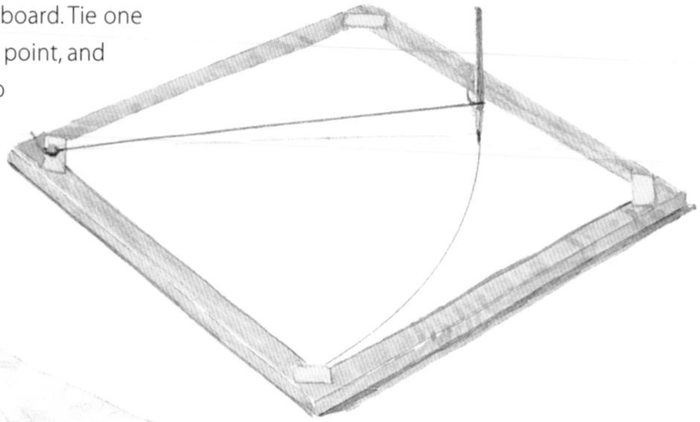

2 Cut out the pattern, then use it as a guide for cutting out the fabric.

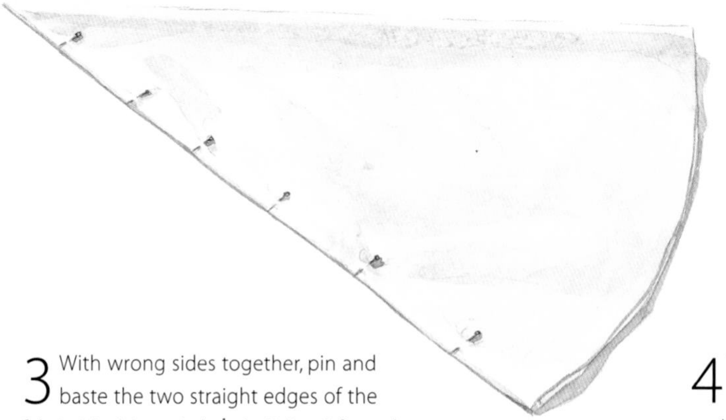

3 With wrong sides together, pin and baste the two straight edges of the fabric. Machine stitch, ½in (1.5cm) from the edge, then trim the seam allowance to ⅛in (3mm) and clip off the surplus fabric at the pointed end.

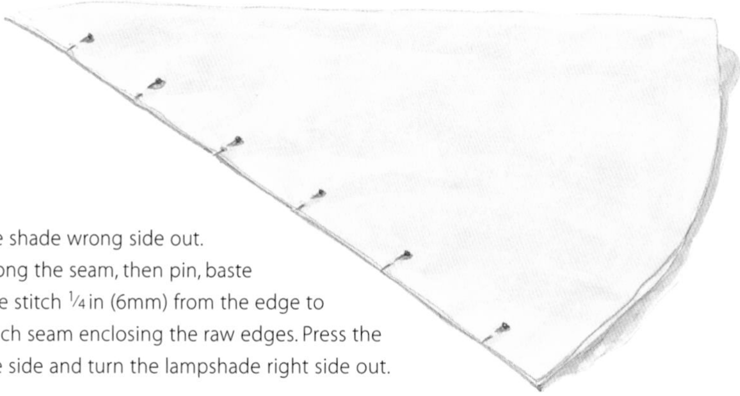

4 Turn the shade wrong side out. Press along the seam, then pin, baste and machine stitch ¼in (6mm) from the edge to make a French seam enclosing the raw edges. Press the seam to one side and turn the lampshade right side out.

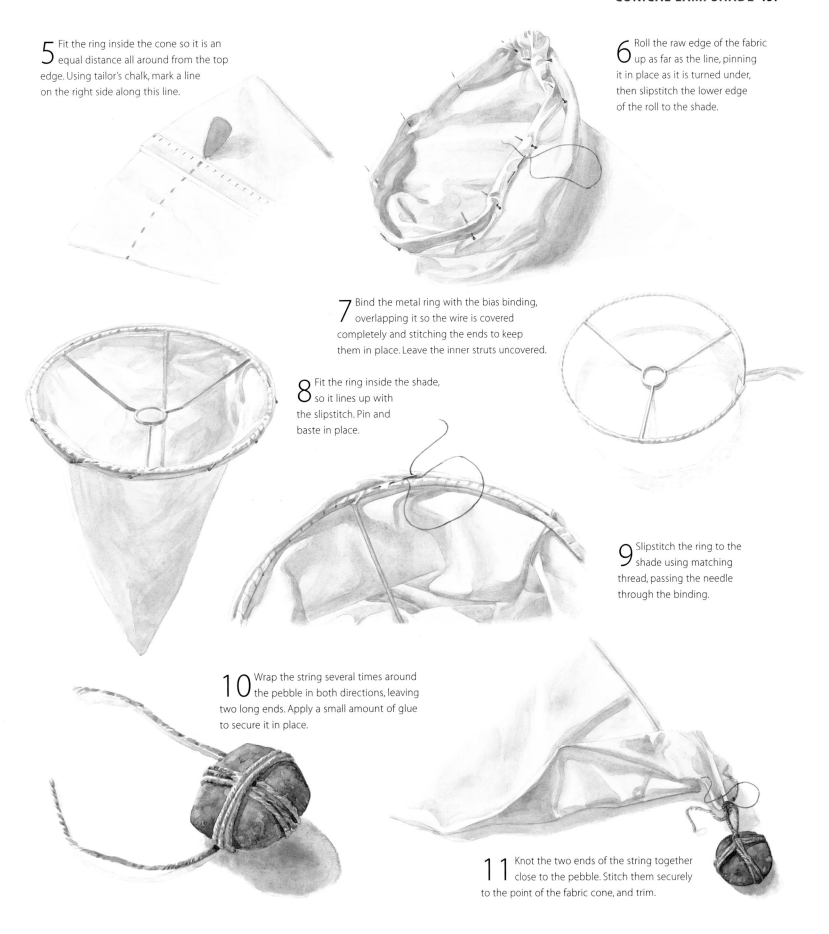

5 Fit the ring inside the cone so it is an equal distance all around from the top edge. Using tailor's chalk, mark a line on the right side along this line.

6 Roll the raw edge of the fabric up as far as the line, pinning it in place as it is turned under, then slipstitch the lower edge of the roll to the shade.

7 Bind the metal ring with the bias binding, overlapping it so the wire is covered completely and stitching the ends to keep them in place. Leave the inner struts uncovered.

8 Fit the ring inside the shade, so it lines up with the slipstitch. Pin and baste in place.

9 Slipstitch the ring to the shade using matching thread, passing the needle through the binding.

10 Wrap the string several times around the pebble in both directions, leaving two long ends. Apply a small amount of glue to secure it in place.

11 Knot the two ends of the string together close to the pebble. Stitch them securely to the point of the fabric cone, and trim.

fabric basket

A square base and four rectangular sides cut from heavy cardboard are enclosed between two squares of blue gingham to make this shallow box. The size and shape could easily be varied by altering the proportions of the pieces, to make it deeper or longer.

Materials and equipment

16 x 48in (40 x 120cm) cotton gingham

10 x 20in (25 x 50cm) cardboard $^{1}/_{6}$ in (4mm) thick

dressmaker's scissors

craft knife

metal ruler

cutting mat

tailor's chalk

matching sewing thread

basic sewing kit

Cutting out from gingham	**Cutting out from cardboard**
Front and back (cut two)	*Base (cut one)*
14in (36cm) square	8in (20cm) square
Ties (cut eight)	*Sides (cut four)*
width = 1$^{1}/_{2}$in (4cm)	width = 2in (5cm)
length = 10in (25cm)	length = 8in (20cm)

Available from Sasha Waddell

1 Press under a $^{3}/_{4}$in (2cm) hem around each edge of the front and back cover.

2 Using tailor's chalk, mark and rule four lines on the right side of the front cover 2$^{1}/_{2}$in (6cm) in from each folded edge.

4 Slip the cardboard base between the basting to check that it fits snugly, then remove it and machine stitch along the two basted lines.

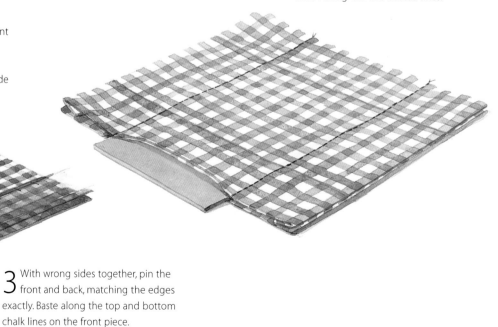

3 With wrong sides together, pin the front and back, matching the edges exactly. Baste along the top and bottom chalk lines on the front piece.

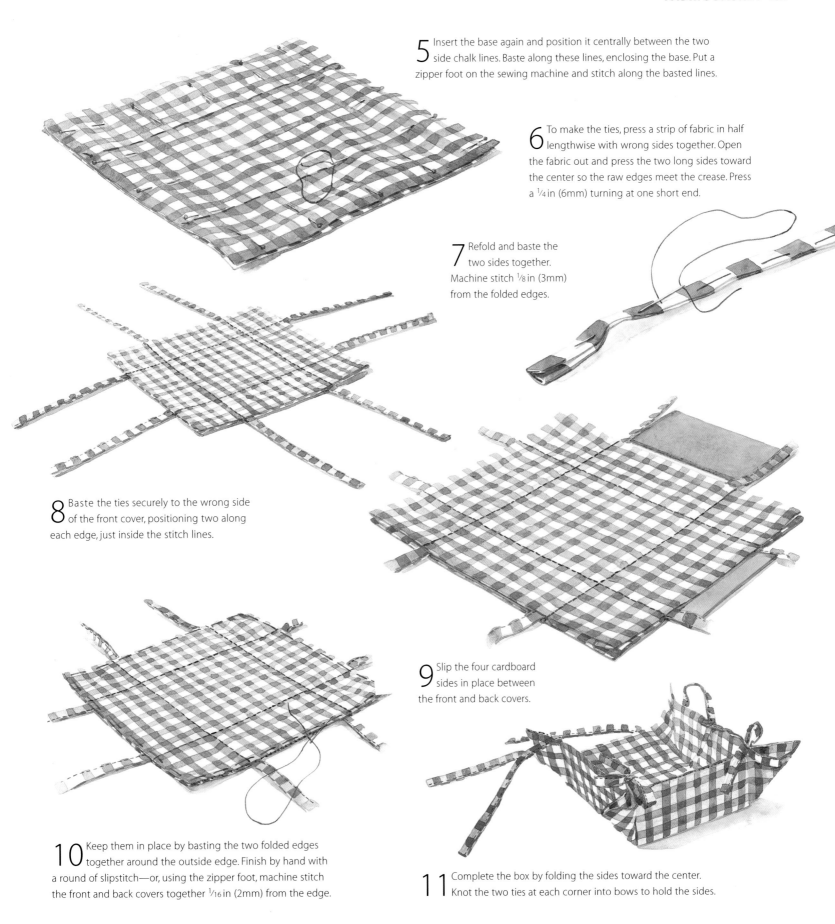

5 Insert the base again and position it centrally between the two side chalk lines. Baste along these lines, enclosing the base. Put a zipper foot on the sewing machine and stitch along the basted lines.

6 To make the ties, press a strip of fabric in half lengthwise with wrong sides together. Open the fabric out and press the two long sides toward the center so the raw edges meet the crease. Press a ¼ in (6mm) turning at one short end.

7 Refold and baste the two sides together. Machine stitch ⅛ in (3mm) from the folded edges.

8 Baste the ties securely to the wrong side of the front cover, positioning two along each edge, just inside the stitch lines.

9 Slip the four cardboard sides in place between the front and back covers.

10 Keep them in place by basting the two folded edges together around the outside edge. Finish by hand with a round of slipstitch—or, using the zipper foot, machine stitch the front and back covers together ¹⁄₁₆ in (2mm) from the edge.

11 Complete the box by folding the sides toward the center. Knot the two ties at each corner into bows to hold the sides.

Directory of suppliers

Retailers If no street address is given for a particular retailer, call or go to website for local stores. **To the trade** Items sold through designers and architects only. **Manufacturers** Items sold to retailers; call or go to website for nearest availability.

GENERAL SUPPLIERS

ABC Carpet & Home
888 Broadway
New York, NY 10003
(212) 473-3000
www.abchome.com
Retailer of fabrics, furniture, bed linens, all home products. One location.

Ballard Designs
1670 Defoor Ave., NW
Atlanta, GA 30318
(800) 367-2775
www.ballarddesigns.com
Retailer. Catalog selling furniture, fabrics, lampshades; custom workroom.

Bloomingdales
1000 Third Avenue
New York, NY 10022
(212) 705-2000
www.bloomingdales.com
Department store. Bed & bath, pillows, decorating department. Twenty-four locations nationwide.

Crate and Barrel
(800) 967-6696
www.crateandbarrel.com
Retailer, catalog. Furniture, bed and bath, accessories. Stores nationwide.

Macy's
(800) BUY-MACY
www.macys.com
Department store. Furniture, bedding, etc. Stores nationwide.

Nieman Marcus
(800) 825-8000
www.neimanmarcus.com
Department store. Furniture, bed and bath, accessories. Thirty-one stores and catalog.

Pierre Deux French Country
870 Madison Avenue
New York, NY 10021
(212) 570-9343
www.pierredeux.com
Retailer of fabric, furniture, accessories. Nine stores; two to-the-trade showrooms.

Pottery Barn
(800) 838-0944
www.potterybarn.com
Retailer of furniture and bed and bath accessories. Stores nationwide. Catalog.

BED LINENS

Ad Hoc Softwares
136 Wooster Street
New York, NY 10012
(212) 982-7703
Local retailer of imported bed linens in natural fabrics.

Aria Fine Linens
214 Park Avenue South
Winter Park, FL 32789
(407) 628-2021
Local retailer.

Bed, Bath and Beyond
(800) GO-BEYOND
www.bedbathandbeyond.com
Retailer with stores nationwide. Catalog.

Bella Linea Nashville
6031 Highway 100
Westgate Shopping Center
Nashville, TN 37205
(615) 352-4041
Local retailer.

Calvin Klein Home
(800) 294-7978
Manufacturer of bed and bath items.

Chambers
Mail-order Department
P.O. Box 7841
San Francisco, CA 94120
(800) 334-9790
Catalog. Elegant, expensive linens, furniture, accessories for bed and bath.

Fortunoff
The Mall at the Source
1300 Old Country Road
Westbury, NY 11590
(516) 832-9000
www.fortunoff.com
Retailer, catalog.

Garnet Hill
231 Main Street
Franconia, NH 03580
(800) 622-6216
www.garnethill.com
Manufacturer of natural-fiber bedding. Catalog.

Gracious Home
1992 Broadway
New York, NY 10023
(212) 231-7800
www.gracioushome.com
Retailer of bed and bath items and pillows. Two Manhattan locations.

Harmony
(800) 869-3446
www.gaiam.com
Manufacturer, catalog. All-natural products for the home.

Lassiter's Bed & Boudoir
3500 Peachtree Road
Atlanta, GA 30326
(404) 261-0765
Local retailer.

Linens Limited Inc.
113 Clay Avenue
Lexington, KY 40502
(888) 3-LINENS,
www.linenslimited.com
Retailer.

CURTAINS AND WINDOW TREATMENTS

Martin Albert Interiors
9 East 19th Street
New York, NY 10003
(212) 673-8000
To the trade. Custom window treatments, upholstery, fabric.

Country Curtains
At the Red Lion Inn
Dept. 2816
Stockbridge
MA 01262
(800) 937-1237

www.countrycurtains.com
Retailer, catalog. Fabrics, window treatments, and home accessories. Stores mostly in East of the U.S.A.

Gige Interiors Ltd.
170 South Main Street
Yardley, PA 19067
(215) 493-8052
Retailer of custom-made window treatments.

Hunter Douglas
One Duette Way
Broomfield, CO 80020
(888) 501-8364
www.hunterdouglas.com
Manufacturer of all kinds of shades and window treatments.

Kirsch
P.O. Box 0370
Sturgis, MI 49091
(800) 528-1407
Manufacturer of curtain and drapery hardware and rods.

Marc Tash Interiors
Brooklyn, NY
(800) MARC-TASH
Retailer of custom drapery, window treatments, upholstery, and slipcovers.

Renovators Supply
Renovators Old Mill
Millers Falls, MA 01349
(800) 659-2211
Manufacturer, retailer, catalog. Window and curtain hardware. Stores in New England.

Smith & Noble
P.O. Box 1387
Corona, CA 91718
(800) 560-0027
www.smithandnoble.com
Retailer, catalog. All kinds of shades and window treatments.

The Warm Co.
954 East Union
Seattle, WA 98122
(800) 234-9276
Manufacturer of insulated fabric for window shades.

www.shadeambition.com
Davis, CA
(800) 838-5442
Manufacturer and online retailer of minishades.

FABRICS AND UPHOLSTERED FURNITURE

Anichini
466 North Robertson Blvd.
Los Angeles, CA 90048
(800) 553-5309
www.anichini.com
Manufacturer of fabrics, decorative pillows, and upholstered sofas and chairs.

B & B Italia USA Inc
150 East 58th Street
New York, NY 10155
(800) 872-1697
www.bebitalia.it
Manufacturer of high-style contemporary furniture.

B & J Fabrics
263 West 40th Street
New York, NY 10018
(212) 354-8150
Local retailer. Natural-fiber fabrics.

Baranzelli Home
1127 Second Avenue
New York, NY 10022
(212) 753-6511
Local retailer. High-quality fabric and trimmings.

Bechenstein's Home Fabrics
4 West 20th Street
New York, NY 10011
(212) 366-5142
Local retailer.

Brunschwig & Fils
979 Third Avenue
New York, NY 10022
(212) 838-7878
www.brunschwig.com
Fabrics and furniture sold to the trade. Nineteen showrooms worldwide.

Calico Corners
203 Gale Lane
Kennett Square, PA 19348
(800) 213-6366
www.calicocorners.com
Retailer of fabric from manufacturers such as Waverly, Ralph Lauren, and furniture. Many stores nationwide.

Donghia Home Furnishings
979 Third Avenue
New York, NY 10022
(800) DONGHIA
www.donghia.com
To the trade. Fabrics and furniture. Showrooms nationwide.

Classic Leather
P.O. Box 2404
Hickory, NC 28603
(828) 328-2046
www.classic-leather.com
Manufacturer of leather-upholstered furniture.

Dualoy Inc
45 West 34th Street
New York, NY 10011
(212) 594-3360
Local retailer. Large selection of hides for upholstery and interiors.

The Fabric Center
485 Electric Avenue
Fitchburg, MA 01420
(508) 343-4402
Retailer of decorator fabrics at discount prices.

Inter-Coastal Textile
480 Broadway
New York, NY 10013
*Retailer of decorative
fabrics at a discount.*

Keepsake Quilting
Route 25B
P.O. Box 1618
Center Harbor
NH 03226-1618
(800) 865-9458
*Retailer of fabrics
and threads.*

Kravet Fabrics Inc.
225 Central Avenue South
Bethpage, NY 11714
(888) 4-KRAVET
www.kravet.com
*Manufacturer selling
fabrics to the trade.*

Oppenheim's
P.O. Box 29
120 East Main Street
North Manchester
IN 46962-0052
(800) 461-6728
*Retailer. Country prints, denim,
chambray, flannel fabrics,
and mill remnants.*

Silk Trading Co.
360 South La Brea Avenue
Los Angeles, CA 90036
(800) 854-0396, or visit
www.silktrading.com
*Retailer and catalog. More than
2,000 silk fabrics, from taffeta to
classic damask, ready-made
curtains, trimmings, lampshades.
Nine stores nationwide.*

VW Home
333 West 39th Street, 10th Floor
New York, NY 10036
(212) 224-5008
*Retail store of leading interior
designer Vincente Wolf Fabrics
and furniture.*

Pauline Yeats
26 East 22nd Street
New York, NY 10003
(212) 228-5353
*Retailer of designer
furniture and fabrics.*

LAMPSHADES
Just Shades
21 Spring Street
New York, NY 10012
(212) 966 2757
Local retailer.

The Lampshade Shop
(661) 327-2145
www.lampshadeshop.com
*Manufacturer and retailer of
custom shades and supplies
for making all kinds of shades.*

Mainely Shades
100 Gray Road
Falmouth, ME 04105
(207) 797 7568
Local retailer.

Oriental Lampshade Co.
816 Lexington Avenue
New York, NY 10021
(212) 832 8190
Retailer.

Ruth Vitow
155 East 56th Street
New York, NY 10022
(212) 355 6616
Local retailer.

PILLOWS
Arts & Crafts Period Textiles
Oakland, CA
(510) 654-1645
*Local retailer of
decorative pillows.*

DJC Design Studio
(800) 554-7890
www.djcDESIGN.com
*Manufacturer of decorative
pillows and throws.*

Dransfield and Ross
New York, NY
(212) 741-7278
*Local retailer of
decorative pillows.*

Michaelian & Kohlberg
225 7th Avenue East
Hendersonville, NC 28792
(800) 258-3977 x10
www.mkhome.com
*Manufacturer of
decorative pillows.*

Pillow Finery
979 Third Avenue
New York, NY 10022
(212) 752 9603
Local retailer.

The Pillowry
P.O. Box 6902
New York, NY 10128
(212) 308 1630
*Retail and to the trade.
By appointment only.*

Susan Sargent
Pawlet, VT
(800) 245-4767
www.susansargent.com
*Manufacturer of bedding
and pillows.*

TRIMMINGS
Clothilde Inc.
2 Sew Smart Way
Stevens Point
WI 54481-8031
(800) 772-2891
*Retailer of discounted
notions, trims, and threads.*

Conso Products
P.O. Box 326
Union, SC 29379
(800) 845-2431
*Manufacturer of decorative
trims, tassels, and fringes.*

Hollywood Trims
Prym-Dritz Corp.
P.O. Box 5028
Spartanburg, SC 29304
(800) 845-4948
*Manufacturer of rayon, cotton,
and metallic trims, cords,
tassels, and thread.*

Houlès Inc.
979 Third Avenue
New York, NY 10022
(212) 935-3900
*Luxurious handmade imported
trims sold to the trade.
Showrooms nationwide.*

Lou Lou Buttons
69 West 38th Street
New York, NY 10018
(212) 398 5498
Local retailer.

Nancy's Notions
P.O. Box 683
Beaver Dam, WI 53916
(800) 833-0690
*Retailer of notions, trims,
and threads.*

C. M. Offray & Sons Inc.
Route 24
P. O. Box 601
Chester, NJ 07930
(908) 879-4700
*Manufacturer of woven and
wire-edge ribbons, flowers,
and bows.*

Tinsel Trading Co.
47 West 38th Street
New York, NY 10018
(212) 730-1030
*Retailer of vintage to
contemporary trims, tassels,
flowers, fringes, buttons, cords,
metallics, and military trims.*

Architects and designers whose work is featured in this book

Ash Sakula Architects
Studio 115
38 Mount Pleasant
London WC1X 0AN
+44 20 7837 9735
Pages 1, 67 al

Benchmark Group plc
25 Sackville Street
London W1
Pages 9, 18-19, 26 & 27 l,
79 bl, 98 l, 122 ar & br

Charlotte Barnes Interiors
26 Stanhope Gardens
London SW7 5QX
Pages 70 l

JoAnn Barwick
Interior Designer
P.O. Box 982
Boca Grande, FL 33921
Pages 38 br, 114-115

Bilhuber Inc.
330 East 59th Street
6th floor
New York, NY 10022
(212) 308-4888
Pages 92 al, 110-111

Blakes Lodging
77 Pantigo Road
East Hampton
New York, NY 11937
(631) 324-1815
www.picket.com
Pages 59, 66 l, 79 bc, 84,
132-133, 148

Laura Bohn Design
30 West 26th Street
New York, NY 10010
(212) 645-3636
www.laurabohndesign.
    com
Pages 13 r, 22-23, 45,
86 b, 87 br, 92 bl, 122, bl,
137, 164

Ann Boyd Design Ltd
33 Elystan Street
London SW3 3NT
+44 20 7591 0202
Pages 15 al, 76 bc, 86 cr,
87 l, 111 a

Nancy Braithwaite Interiors
2300 Peachtree Road
Atlanta, GA 30309
Page 64

Sabina Fay Braxton
Cloth of Gold
Grennan Watermill
Thomastown
Co Kilkenny
Ireland
+353 565 4383

by appointment in New York:
(212) 535 2587

by appointment in Paris:
+33 1 4657 11 62
Pages 25 r, 68 a, 71 a,
82 a, 86 a & cl, 94 b, 103 al,
142 a

Clive Butcher Designs
The Granary
The Quay
Wivenhoe
Essex CO7 9BU
+44 1206 827708
Page 138

Piero Castellini Baldissera
Studio Castellini
Via Morozzo della Rocco, 5
20123 Milan
Italy
Pages 97 a

David Collins
    Architecture & Design
Unit 6 & 7
Chelsea Wharf
Lots Road
London SW10 0QJ
+44 20 7349-5900
Pages 27 ar, 74, 83 al, 98 r

Conner Prairie Musuem
134000 Alisonville Road
Fishers, IN 46038
Page 128 l

Chris Cowper
Cowper Griffith Associates
Chartered Architects
15 High Street
Whittlesford
Cambridge CB2 4LT
Page 129 r

Jo Crepain
    Architect
Vlaandernstraat 6
8-2000 Antwerp
Belgium
+32 3 213-61-61
Page 93 bl

CR Studio Architects, PC
6 West 18th Street
9th floor
New York, NY 10011
212 989-8187
www.crstudio.com
Pages 34, 76 bl, 77, 79 ar &
br, 99 al & r, 122 al

John Cullen Lighting
585 King's Road
London SW6 2EH
+44 20 7371-5400
Page 103, ar

De Le Cuona Textile and
    Home Collection
Head Office:
9-10 Osborne Mews
Windsor
Berks SL4 3DE

Retail outlet:
De Le Cuona, 1st fl.
The General Trading Co.
2 Symons Street
London SW3 2TJ
www.delecuona.co.uk
Pages 15 bl, 16 l, 80 br,
90 cc, 139 l

Mary Drysdale
1733 Connecticut Avenue
    NW,
Washington DC 20009
Pages 11 a, 150 r, 152, 168

Ecomusée de la Grande
    Lande
Marquèze
40630 Sabres
Bordeaux, France
Page 131

Han Feng
Fashion designer
333 West 39 Street, 12th fl.
New York, NY 10018
(212) 695-9509
Page 140 bl & br

Ken Foreman
    Architect
105 Duane Street
New York, NY 10007
(212) 924-4503
Pages 35, 68 b, 83 ac & ar,
108 l & 108-109

Mark Gillette
    Interior Design
The Barn
Elthorns Farm
Denhall Lane
Burton
South Wirral
Cheshire CH64 5SA
+44 151 336 3528
Pages 27 cr, 65 a
*Favours the use of natural,
textured surfaces and
finishes including limestone,
oak, linen and suede.*

Zina Glazebrook
ZG DESIGN
10 Wireless Road
East Hampton
NY 11937
(631) 329-7486
www.zgdesign.com
Page 75 al

James Gorst Architects
35 Lambs Conduit Street
London WC1N 3NG
+44 20 7831 8300
Pages 119 b, 10 l

Wendy Harrop
Interior Designer
11 Rectory Road
London SW13 0DU
Pages 50-51 67 br, 112,
126 a

Hi-Tex Inc.
Crypton Super Fabric
32813 Middlebelt
Farmington Hills
MI 48334
(800) CRYPTON
www.cryptonfabric.com
Pages 34, 76 bl, 77, 79 ar &
br, 99 al & r, 122 al

John C Hope
    Architects
3 St Bernard's Crescent
Edinburgh EH4 1NR
+44 131 315-2215
Page 123 l

Interni Pty Ltd
Interior Design
    Consultancy
15-19 Boundary Street
Rushcutter's Bay
Sydney 2010
Australia
Page 63

IPL Interiors
François Gilles and
Dominique Lubar
Unit 26C1
Thames House
140 Battersea Park Road
London SW11 4NY
+44 20 7622-3009
Page 127

Jacomini
    Interior Design
1701 Brun
Suite 101
Houston, TX
Pages 96 ar, 126 b

Joanna Jefferson
    Architects
222 Oving Road
Chichester
West Sussex PO19 4EJ
+44 1243 532398
jjeffearch@aol.com
Page 123 r

Johnson Naylor
13 Britton Street
London EC1M 5SX
+44 20 7490 8885
Page 90 cl

McDowell + Benedetti
    Architects
62 Rosebery Avenue
London EC1R 4RR
+44 20 7278 8810
McDowellBenedetti.com
Page 69

MODÉNATURE
Créations Henry Becq
3, rue Jacob
    et 59, rue de Seine
75006 Paris, France
Pages 29 al & br, 56, 80 a,
106 & 107 a, 118, 135 bl,
c & r, 184

Lynn Morgan Design
19 Hilltop Road
Norwalk
CT 06854
(203) 854-5037
Pages 12-13, 36-37, 38 bl,
95 b, 117, 146-147

Claire Nelson
Nelson Design
169 St Johns Hill
London SW11 1TQ
+44 20 7924 4542
Pages 9, 18-19, 26 & 27 l, 79
bl, 98 l, 122 ar & br

Roger Oates Design
Shop & Showroom:
1 Munro Terrace
off Cheyne Walk
London SW10 0DL

Studio shop:
The Long Barn
Eastnor
Ledbury
Herefordshire HR8 1EL

*Rugs and runners
mail order catalogue:*
+44 1531 631611
Pages 10 r, 15 al, 30 al,
72 l, 121, 140 ar, 141

Ogawa/Depardon
    Architects
137 Varick Street, #404
New York
NY 10013
(212) 627 7390
Page 55

OKA Direct
A unique collection of mail order furniture and home accessories including rattan, painted furniture, leather and horn.
For a catalogue, please call +44 870 160 6002
www.okadirect.com
Pages 27 br, 29 bl, 54 b, 83 br, 103 b, 120, 134 & 135 a, 192

Andrew Parr
SJB Interior Design Pty Ltd.
Studio Southbank
5 Haig Street
South Melbourne 3205
Australia
Page 62 l

Caroline Paterson
Paterson Gornall Interiors
50 Lavender Gardens
London SW11 1DN
+44 20 7738 2530
Pages 92 br, 138

Plain English
Kitchen Design
The Tannery
Coombs
Stowmarket
Suffolk IP14 2EN
Page 129 bl

Lena Proudlock
Furniture Design 12
Gloucestershire GL8 8UN
Page 125 l

Mark Pynn A.I.A.
McMillen Pynn
 Architecture L.L.P.
P.O. Box 1068
Sun Valley
ID 83353
(208) 622-4656
www.sunvalleyarchitect.
 com
Page 16 r

Reed Creative Services Ltd
151a Sydney Street
London SW3 6NT
+44 20 7565 0066
Pages 15 al, 76 bc, 103 ar, 111 a

Johanne Riss
Stylist, Designer &
 Fashion Designer
35 Place du Nouveau
Marché aux Graens
1000 Brussels
Belgium
+32 2 513 0900
Pages 14, 93 al

Richard Ronald
c/o Manuel Canovas
2 North Terrace
London SW3
Page 7

Steven Ryan
 Design and Decoration
60 Ledbury Road
London W11
Page 44 br

Sheila Scholes, Designer
+44 1480 498241
Pages 5, 28 l, 59 b, 70 r, 80 bl, 81, 88-89, 100 l, 101 l & r, 128 r, 132 a, 144 l, 180

Sequana
64 Avenue de la Motte
 Picquet
75015 Paris, France
+33 1 45 66 58 40
sequana@wanadoo.fr
Pages 20 ac, b & 21, 111 b

Taylor Woodrow Capital
 Developments Ltd
International House
1 St Katherine's Way
London E1 9TW
+44 20 7488 0555
Pages 27 ar, 74, 83 al, 98 r

Todhunter Earle Interiors
Chelsea Reach
1st fl., 79-89 Lots Road
London SW10 0RN
+44 20 7349 9999
www.todhunterearle.com
Pages 29 ar, 61 a, 107 b, 119 a, 144 r

Sasha Waddell
269 Wandsworth Bridge
 Road
London SW6 2TX
+44 20 7736 0766
Pages 2-3, 32 a & b, 39, 59 ar, 65 b, 72 r, 78, 79 al & cl, 90 b, 182

Picture credits

Key: *a* = above, *b* = below, *l* = left, *r* = right, *c* = center

All photographs by David Montgomery unless otherwise stated.

Endpapers photographer Polly Wreford; **1** photographer James Merrell/An apartment in London designed by Ash Sakula Architects; **2-3** Sasha Waddell's house in London; **4** photographer Tom Leighton; **5** Sheila Scholes' house near Cambridge; **7** photographer James Merrell/Richard Ronald's house in London; **8-9** Carlton Gardens apartment in London designed by Claire Nelson at Nelson Design; **10** *l* photographer Andrew Wood/An apartment in London designed by James Gorst; **10** *r* photographer Andrew Wood/Roger Oates & Fay Morgan's house in Eastnor; **11** *a* photographer James Merrell/A house designed by Mary Drysdale; **11** *b* photographer Simon Upton/Carol Reid's apartment in Paris; **12-13** A house in Connecticut designed by Lynn Morgan Design; **13** *r* photographer Fritz von der Schulenburg/A house in Pennsylvania designed by Laura Bohn of Laura Bohn Design Associates; **14** photographer Andrew Wood/Johanne Riss' house in Brussels; **15** *al* photographer James Merrell/Designed by Reed Boyd; **15** *ar* photographer Tom Leighton/Roger Oates & Fay Morgan's house in Eastnor; **15** *bl* photographer Andrew Wood/Bernie de Le Cuona's house in Windsor; **15** *br* photographer James Merrell; **16** *l* photographer Andrew Wood/Bernie de Le Cuona's house in Windsor; **16** *r* photographer Andrew Wood/Philip & Barbara Silver's house in Idaho designed by McMillen Pynn Architecture; **17** photographer James Merrell; **18-19** Carlton Gardens apartment in London designed by Claire Nelson at Nelson Design; **20** *al* photographer Sandra Lane; **20** *ac, b* & **21** photographer Andrew Wood/Mary Shaw's Sequana apartment in Paris; **20** *ar* photographer Tom Leighton; **22-23** Laura Bohn's apartment in New York designed by Laura Bohn Design Associates; **24** *l* & *ar* photographer James Merrell; **24** *br* photographer James Merrell; **25** *l* photographer James Merrell/Liz Dougherty Pierce's home; **25** *r* Sabina Fay Braxton's apartment in Paris; **26** & **27** *l* Carlton Gardens apartment in London designed by Claire Nelson at Nelson Design; **27** *ar* The Montevetro apartment in London designed by David Collins, photographed courtesy of Taylor Woodrow Capital Developments Ltd.; **27** *cr* The Nobilis-Fontan apartment in London designed by Mark Gillette; **27** *br* Annabel Astor's house in London is full of furniture and accessories designed exclusively for her OKA Direct Mail order catalogue; **28** *l* Sheila Scholes' house near Cambridge; **28** *r* & **29** *ar* House in South London designed by Todhunter Earle Interiors; **29** *al* & *br* Designer of Modénature Henry Becq's apartment in Paris; **29** *bl* Annabel Astor's house in London is full of furniture and accessories designed exclusively for her OKA Direct Mail order catalogue; **30** *al* photographer Henry Bourne/Roger Oates & Fay Morgan's house in Eastnor; **30** *bl* photographer Simon Upton; **30** *r* photographer James Merrell/Høyersten family house on western fiord in Norway; **31** *al, ac, bl* & *br* photographer James Merrell; **31** *ar* photographer Henry Bourne; **32** *a* & *b* Sasha Waddell's house in London; **33** photographer James Merrell/Hotel Villa Gallici Aix en Provence, France; **34** The House of Crypton living laboratory apartment showroom in New York City designed by CR Studio Architects, PC; **35** An apartment in New York designed by Ken Foreman; **36-37** A house in Connecticut designed by Lynn Morgan Design; **38** *bl* A house in Connecticut designed by Lynn Morgan Design; **38** *a* photographer Polly Wreford/The Sawmills Studios; **38** *br* photographer Simon Upton/JoAnn Barwick & Fred Berger's house in New Preston, Connecticut; **39** Sasha Waddell's house in London; **40** *a* & *b* photographer Tom Leighton; **41** *a* photographer Polly Wreford; **41** *bl* photographer Polly Wreford/Mary Foley's house in Connecticut; **41** *br* photographer Polly Wreford; **42-43** photographer James Merrell/Hotel de la Mirande, Avignon; **44** *al* & *bl* photographer James Merrell/Ngila Boyd, London; **44** *ar* photographer James Merrell/Hotel Villa Gallici Aix en Provence, France; **44** *br* photographer James Merrell/Interior Design by Stephen Ryan Design & Decoration; **45** Laura Bohn's apartment in New York designed by Laura Bohn Design Associates; **46** photographer James Merrell/Hotel Villa Gallici Aix en Provence, France; **47** & **48** photographer James Merrell/Hotel de la Mirande, Avignon; **49** & **50** *l* photographer James Merrell; **50-51** photographer Simon Upton/Wendy Harrop's cottage in Wiltshire; **52-53** photographer Tom Leighton; **54** *a* photographer James Merrell/Curtain design Mary Bright; **54** *b* Annabel Astor's house in London is full of furniture and accessories designed exclusively for her OKA Direct Mail order catalogue; **55** photographer James Merrell/Architect Ogawa Depardon, curtain design Mary Bright; **56** Designer of Modénature Henry Becq's apartment in Paris; **57** *l* photographer James Merrell/Hotel de la Mirande, Avignon; **57** *ar* & *br* photographer

James Merrell; **58** *a* photographer James Merrell; **59** *b* photographer Simon Upton/Maison d'Hôte; **59** Blakes Lodging designed by Jeanie Blake www.picket.com/blakesBB/blakes.htm; **59** *ar* Sasha Waddell's house in London; **59** *b* Sheila Scholes' house near Cambridge; **60** *bl* & **60-61** photographer James Merrell; **61** *a* House in South London designed by Todhunter Earle Interiors; **62** *l* photographer James Merrell/Andrew Parr's house in Melbourne; **62** *r* photographer Henry Bourne; **63** photographer James Merrell/A house in Sydney designed by Interni Interior Design Consultancy; **64** photographer Simon Upton/Nancy Braithwaite Interiors; **65** *a* the Nobilis-Fontan apartment in London designed by Mark Gillette; **65** *b* Sasha Waddell's house in London; **66** *l* Blakes Lodging designed by Jeanie Blake www.picket.com/blakesBB/blakes.htm; **66** *r* photographer Ray Main/Nello Renault's loft in Paris; **67** *al* photographer Ray Main; **67** *ar* photographer James Merrell/An apartment in London designed by Ash Sakula Architects; **67** *bl* photographer Simon Upton/Mr & Mrs Ruttenberg's house in Pennsylvania; **67** *br* photographer Simon Upton/Wendy Harrop's cottage in Wiltshire; **68** *a* Sabina Fay Braxton's apartment in Paris; **68** *b* An apartment in New York designed by Ken Foreman; **69** photographer Ray Main/David & Claudia Dorrell's apartment in London designed in conjunction with McDowell + Benedetti; **70** *l* photographer James Merrell/Designer Charlotte Barnes; **70** *r* Sheila Scholes' house near Cambridge; **71** *a* Sabina Fay Braxton's apartment in Paris; **71** *b* photographer Fritz von der Schulenburg/Jason McCoy's apartment in New York; **72** *l* photographer Tom Leighton/ Roger Oates & Fay Morgan's house in Eastnor; **72** *r* Sasha Waddell's house in London; **73** photographer Polly Wreford/Kimberly Watson's house in London; **74** The Montevetro apartment in London designed by David Collins, photographed courtesy of Taylor Woodrow Capital Developments Ltd; **75** *al* photographer Ray Main/Client's residence, East Hampton, New York, designed by ZG DESIGN; **75** *ar* photographer James Merrell; **75** *br* photographer Henry Bourne; **76** *a* photographer Tom Leighton; **76** *bl* The House of Crypton living laboratory apartment showroom in New York City designed by CR Studio Architects, PC; **76** *bc* photographer Tom Leighton/Keith Varty & Alan Cleaver's apartment in London designed by Jonathan Reed/Reed Boyd; **76** *br* photographer Tom Leighton/Arne Maynard; **77** The House of Crypton living laboratory apartment showroom in New York City designed by CR Studio Architects, PC; **78, 79** *al* & *cl* Sasha Waddell's house in London; **79** *bl* Carlton Gardens apartment in London designed by Claire Nelson at Nelson Design; **79** *bc* Blakes Lodging designed by Jeanie Blake www.picket.com/blakesBB/blakes.htm; **79** *ar* & *br* The House of Crypton living laboratory apartment showroom in New York City designed by CR Studio Architects, PC; **80** *a* Designer of Modénature Henry Becq's apartment in Paris; **80** *bl* Sheila Scholes' house near Cambridge; **80** *br* photographer Andrew Wood/Bernie de Le Cuona's house in Windsor; **81** Sheila Scholes' house near Cambridge; **82** *a* Sabina Fay Braxton's apartment in Paris; **82** *b* photographer James Merrell; **83** *al* The Montevetro apartment in London designed by David Collins, photographed courtesy of Taylor Woodrow Capital Developments Ltd; **83** *ac* & *ar* An apartment in New York designed by Ken Foreman; **83** *bl* photographer Polly Wreford/Ros Fairman's house in London; **83** *br* Annabel Astor's house in London is full of furniture and accessories designed exclusively for her OKA Direct Mail order catalogue; **84** Blakes Lodging designed by Jeanie Blake www.picket.com/blakesBB/blakes.htm; **85** *l* photographer Polly Wreford/Adria Ellis' apartment in New York; **85** *r* photographer James Merrell; **86** *a* & *cl* Sabina Fay Braxton's apartment in Paris; **86** *b* Laura Bohn's apartment in New York designed by Laura Bohn Design Associates; **86** *cr* & **87** *l* photographer James Merrell/Anne Boyd; **87** *ar* photographer Tom Leighton; **87** *br* Laura Bohn's apartment in New York designed by Laura Bohn Design Associates; **88-89** Sheila Scholes' house near Cambridge; **90** *a* photographer James Merrell/Janie Jackson, Stylist/Desginer; **90** *cl* photographer Andrew Wood/Roger & Suzy Black's apartment in London designed by Johnson Naylor; **90** *c* photographer Andrew

Wood/Bernie de Le Cuona's house in Windsor; **90** *cr* photographer James Merrell; **90** *b* Sasha Waddell's house in London; **91** *a* photographer Henry Bourne; **91** *b* photographer Polly Wreford; **92** *al* photographer Ray Main/A house in Pennsylvania designed by Jeffrey Bilhuber; **92** *bl* photographer Fritz von der Schulenburg/A house in Pennsylvania designed by Laura Bohn of Laura Bohn Design Associates; **92** *br* photographer Fritz von der Schulenburg/Philippa Rose's apartment in London designed by Caroline Paterson with furniture supplied by Leonie Lee of Snap Dragon; **93** *al* photographer Andrew Wood/Johanne Riss' house in Brussels; **93** *bl* photographer Andrew Wood/Architect Jo Crepain; **93** *r* photographer James Merrell/Janie Jackson, Stylist/Desginer; **94** *a* photographer Simon Upton; **94** *b* Sabina Fay Braxton's apartment in Paris; **95** *a* photographer Henry Bourne/Ellen O'Neill, Sag Harbour, New York; **95** *b* A house in Connecticut designed by Lynn Morgan Design; **96** *al* & *bl* photographer James Merrell; **96** *ar* photographer Simon Upton/Jacomini Interior Design; **97** *a* photographer Fritz von der Schulenburg/Piero Castellini Baldissera's house in Montalcino, Siena; **97** *b* photographer James Merrell; **98** *l* Carlton Gardens apartment in London designed by Claire Nelson at Nelson Design; **98** *r* The Montevetro apartment in London designed by David Collins, photographed courtesy of Taylor Woodrow Capital Developments Ltd; **99** *al* & *r* The House of Crypton living laboratory apartment showroom in New York City designed by CR Studio Architects, PC; **99** *b* photographer James Merrell; **100** *l*, **101** *l* & *r* Sheila Scholes' house near Cambridge; **100** *r* photographer Sandra Lane; **102** photographer James Merrell; **103** *al* Sabina Fay Braxton's apartment in Paris; **103** *ar* photographer Ray Main/Jonathan Reed's apartment in London, lighting designed by Sally Storey, Design Director of John Cullen Lighting; **103** *b* Annabel Astor's house in London is full of furniture and accessories designed exclusively for her OKA Direct Mail order catalogue; **104-105** photographer Andrew Wood/Gabriele Sanders' apartment in New York; **106** & **107** *a* Designer of Modénature Henry Becq's apartment in Paris; **107** *b* House in South London designed by Todhunter Earle Interiors; **108** *l* & **108-109** An apartment in New York designed by Ken Foreman; **110-111** photographer Ray Main/A house in Pennsylvania designed by Jeffrey Bilhuber; **111** *a* photographer James Merrell/Keith Varty & Alan Cleaver's apartment in London designed by Jonathan Reed/Reed & Boyd; **111** *b* photographer Andrew Wood/Mary Shaw's Sequana apartment in Paris; **112** photographer Simon Upton/ Wendy Harrop's cottage in Wiltshire; **113** Zara Colchester's house in London; **114-115** photographer Simon Upton/JoAnn Barwick & Fred Berger's house in New Preston, Connecticut; **115** *r* & **116** photographer Henry Bourne; **117** A house in Connecticut designed by Lynn Morgan Design; **118** Designer of Modénature Henry Becq's apartment in Paris; **119** *a* House in South London designed by Todhunter Earle Interiors; **119** *b* photographer Andrew Wood/an apartment in London designed by James Gorst; **120** Annabel Astor's house in London is full of furniture and accessories designed exclusively for her OKA Direct Mail order catalogue; **121** photographer Andrew Wood/Roger Oates & Fay Morgan's house in Eastnor; **122** *al* The House of Crypton living laboratory apartment showroom in New York City designed by CR Studio Architects, PC; **122** *bl* Laura Bohn's apartment in New York designed by Laura Bohn Design Associates; **122** *ar* & *br* Carlton Gardens apartment in London designed by Claire Nelson at Nelson Design; **123** *l* photographer Ray Main/Robert Callender & Elizabeth Ogilvie's studio in Fife designed by John C Hope Architects; **123** *r* photographer Ray Main/Marina & Peter Hill's barn in West Sussex designed by Marina Hill, Peter James Construction Management, Chichester, The West Sussex Antique Timber Company, Wisborough Green, and Joanna Jefferson Architects; **124** photographer James Merrell/ Gabriele Sanders' apartment in New York; **125** *l* photographer Polly Wreford/Lena Proudlock's house in Gloucestershire; **125** *r* photographer Polly Wreford/Kimberly Watson's house in London; **126** *a* photographer Simon Upton/

Wendy Harrop's cottage in Wiltshire; **126** *b* photographer Simon Upton/Jacomini Interior Design; **127** photographer Simon Upton/A house in Tangier designed by François Gilles of IPL Interiors; **128** *l* photographer Simon Upton/Conner Prairie Museum; **128** *r* Sheila Scholes' house near Cambridge; **129** *a* photographer Tom Leighton; **129** *bl* photographer Simon Upton/A kitchen designed by Plain English; **129** *r* photographer Simon Upton/ A house in Norfolk designed by Chris Cowper of Cowper Griffith Associates, Chartered Architects; **130** photographer Henry Bourne; **131** photographer Simon Upton/Ecomusée de la Grande Lande; **131** *b* photographer James Merrell/Høyersten family house on western fiord in Norway; **132** *a* Sheila Scholes' house near Cambridge; **132** *b* & **132-133** Blakes Lodging designed by Jeanie Blake www.picket.com/blakesBB/blakes.htm; **134** & **135** *a* Annabel Astor's house in London is full of furniture and accessories designed exclusively for her OKA Direct Mail order catalogue; **135** *bl*, *c* & *r* Designer of Modénature Henry Becq's apartment in Paris; **136** photographer Andrew Wood/Dawna and Jerry Walter's house in London; **137** Laura Bohn's apartment in New York designed by Laura Bohn Design Associates; **138** photographer Chris Everard/Philippa Rose's house in London designed by Caroline Paterson/Victoria Fairfax of Paterson Gornall Interiors, together with Clive Butcher Designs; **139** *l* photographer Andrew Wood/Bernie de Le Cuona's house in Windsor; **139** *r* photographer James Merrell; **140** *ar* photographer Andrew Wood/ Roger Oates & Fay Morgan's house in Eastnor; **140** *bl* & *br* photographer Andrew Wood/Han Feng's apartment in New York designed by Han Feng; **141** photographer Tom Leighton/Roger Oates & Fay Morgan's house in Eastnor; **142** *a* Sabina Fay Braxton's apartment in Paris; **142** *bl*, *br* & **143** photographer James Merrell; **144** *l* Sheila Scholes' house near Cambridge; **144** *r* A house in South London designed by Todhunter Earle Interiors; **145** photographer Simon Upton/Mr & Mrs François von Hurter; **146** *l* photographer Polly Wreford/Mary Foley's house in Connecticut; **146-147** A house in Connecticut designed by Lynn Morgan Design; **148** Blakes Lodging designed by Jeanie Blake www.picket.com/blakesBB/blakes.htm; **149** *a* photographer Pia Tryde; **149** *b* photographer Sandra Lane; **150** *l* photographer James Merrell; **150** *r* photographer James Merrell/A house designed by Mary Drysdale; **151** photographer James Merrell/ Hotel de la Mirande, Avignon; **152** photographer James Merrell/A house designed by Mary Drysdale; **159** photographer James Merrel/Hotel Villa Gallici Aix en Provence, France; **160** photographer Simon Upton; **161** photographer James Merrell; **162** photographer Henry Bourne; **164** Laura Bohn's apartment in New York designed by Laura Bohn Design Associates; **167** photographer James Merrell/Svindersvik, Nacka, Stockholm; **168** photographer James Merrell/A house designed by Mary Drysdale; **172**, **173** & **174** photographer James Merrell; **177** photographer Henry Bourne; **178** photographer James Merrell; **180** Sheila Scholes' house near Cambridge; **182** Sasha Waddell's house in London; **184** Designer of Modénature Henry Becq's apartment in Paris; **192** Annabel Astor's house in London is full of furniture and accessories designed exclusively for her OKA Direct Mail order catalogue

Index